The Community Builder's Journal

Praise for this book

'*The Community Builder's Journal* offers a year of weekly reflections and experiments to help readers strengthen the ties that make communities thrive. Each entry blends story, practice and a shared recipe, turning everyday acts of care into opportunities for connection. Practical and hopeful, it's a resource for communities that want to grow more collaborative, creative and compassionate.'

Andrew Leigh MP, Assistant Minister for Charities and co-author of 'Reconnected: A Community Builder's Handbook'

'*The Community Builder's Journal* is a powerful catalyst for reimagining our connections, inviting us to embrace the transformative potential of community development and place conscious pedagogy. With its thoughtful prompts and practical guidance, it enables us to cultivate belonging in every corner of our lives and local places.'

Cormac Russell, co-author of 'The Connected Community and author of Rekindling Democracy'

'We all know that humans are social creatures who need groups and communities of all kinds – especially local communities – to nurture and sustain us, and to give us that all-important sense of belonging that is so fundamental to our mental and emotional health. And yet, we are suffering epidemics of loneliness, anxiety and depression fuelled by social fragmentation and isolation. What's to be done? With the publication of *The Community Builder's Journal* we now have a solution.

Wise, sane and realistic, this book is a treasure-trove of intensely practical advice for community-building, based on the authors' rich experience.

If you want to be part of a quiet revolution that will improve the mental and emotional health of the nation, start local ... and start with this book.'

Hugh Mackay, social psychologist and author

'*The Community Builder's Journal* is an extraordinary weaving of wisdom, practice, and heart. It honours the deep knowing that true community building is as much about connection and care as it is about method and action. Through stories of lived experience and grounded reflection, this book invites us to pause, listen, and remember what really matters; our shared humanity and the strength that comes from working together. As someone who has walked alongside communities and facilitators around the world, I'm inspired by how this collection embodies the spirit of possibility and reminds us that when we build with, not for, we create lasting change. Used as a daily reflection tool throughout the year, it gently guides readers into deeper thought, meaningful action, and an ever-growing sense of what's possible when we nurture community from the heart and yes, the cookies and the hummus will help.'

Dee Brooks, Jeder Institute, Australia; ABCD Institute, Chicago; and participatory community building practitioner

The Community Builder's Journal

Guided reflections and experiments for your community-building journey

Peter Westoby
Dave Andrews
Howard Buckley
Rachael Donovan
Gerard Dowling
Kirsty Leigh
Richard Warner

Practical Action Publishing Ltd
25 Albert Street, Rugby,
Warwickshire, CV21 2SD, UK
www.practicalactionpublishing.com

© The Community Cooperative Collective, 2025

The author has asserted their right under the Copyright, Designs and Patents Act 1988 to be identified as author of this work.

All rights reserved. No part of this publication may be reprinted or reproduced or utilized in any form or by any electronic, mechanical, or other means, now known or hereafter invented, including photocopying and recording, or in any information storage or retrieval system, without the written permission of the publishers.

Product or corporate names may be trademarks or registered trademarks, and are used only for identification and explanation without intent to infringe.

A catalogue record for this book is available from the British Library.

A catalogue record for this book has been requested from the Library of Congress.

ISBN 978-1-78853-415-4 Paperback

ISBN 978-1-78853-417-8 Electronic book

Citation: The Community Cooperative Collective (2025) *The Community Builder's Journal: Guided reflections and experiments for your community-building journey*, Rugby, UK: Practical Action Publishing http://doi.org/10.3362/9781788534178

Since 1974, Practical Action Publishing has published and disseminated books and information in support of international development work throughout the world.

Practical Action Publishing is a trading name of Practical Action Publishing Ltd (Company Reg. No. 1159018), the wholly owned publishing company of Practical Action. Practical Action Publishing trades only in support of its parent charity objectives and any profits are covenanted back to Practical Action (Charity Reg. No. 247257, Group VAT Registration No. 880 9924 76).

The views and opinions in this publication are those of the author and do not represent those of Practical Action Publishing Ltd or its parent charity Practical Action.

Reasonable efforts have been made to publish reliable data and information, but the author and publisher cannot assume responsibility for the validity of all materials or for the consequences of their use.

Cover illustration by: Fiona Miller
Typesetting and design by: Katarzyna Markowska, Practical Action Publishing

The manufacturer's authorised representative in the EU for product safety is Lightning Source France, 1 Av. Johannes Gutenberg, 78310 Maurepas, France.

compliance@lightningsource.fr

Contents

Foreword ix
Acknowledgements xi
Introduction 1

Part 1
Orienting, Understanding, Building, and Sustaining

Section 1
Orienting ourselves towards community building 13
Entry 1
Time, patience, and space 15
Entry 2
Experimenting with action 19
Entry 3
Noticing community as an emergent phenomenon 23
Entry 4
Start with what's strong, not with what's wrong 27
Entry 5
Relationships matter 31
Recipe
Banana and macadamia granola 35

Section 2
Understanding community 37
Entry 6
What is this 'community' thing, anyway? 39
Entry 7
Vision and values for community 43
Entry 8
Community as social capital 47
Entry 9
The dark side of community 51
Recipe
Aleppo chicken and rice 55

Section 3
Building purposeful connections 57
Entry 10
The importance of timing when making connections with others 59
Entry 11
Go to the people, ask the people, see what the people see 63
Entry 12
Dialogue and holding your agenda lightly 67
Entry 13
Keywords and common themes 73
Recipe
Dips 77

Section 4
Building small groups 79
Entry 14
Small groups: the heartbeat of community 81
Entry 15
Small is beautiful, and inclusion is the key 85
Entry 16
Movement from a private to a shared concern 89
Entry 17
Building small groups through the 0–1–3 method 93
Recipe
Spiced cauliflower salad bowl 97

Section 5
Sustaining groups 99
Entry 18
What sustains groups? 101
Entry 19
Stages of group development 105

Entry 20
Sustaining groups when things
get stuck or conflict arises 111
Entry 21
Allowing groups to die well 115
Recipe
Caramel slice 119

Section 6
Interlude. What hinders your
involvement in
community building? 121
Entry 22
Personal disempowerment 123
Entry 23
Relational disempowerment 127
Entry 24
Structural disempowerment 131
Entry 25
The decline of community in the
modern world 135
Recipe
Tortilla stack 139

Part 2
Pathways of connecting and
change 141

Section 7
Ecological communities 143
Entry 26
Connecting with the natural world 145
Entry 27
Learning from the natural world 149
Entry 28
How to be in a reciprocal
relationship with nature 153
Entry 29
Responding to ecological crisis
with love 157
Recipe
Khulood's falafels 161

Section 8
Economics as if community
matters 163
Entry 30
Economics as if people matter 165
Entry 31
Finding alternatives within the
dominant economy 169
Entry 32
Transforming the local economy 173
Entry 33
Alternative economic models 179
Recipe
Gardener's pie 183

Section 9
Community through a social lens 185
Entry 34
What are the social assets in your
community? 187
Entry 35
The pandemic of social isolation:
looking out for the lonely 191
Entry 36
Exclusion, inclusion, and solidarity 195
Entry 37
Identity as a vehicle for division
or connection 199
Recipe
Vietnamese-style rice paper rolls 203

Section 10
Culture and cultural change 205
Entry 38
Cultivating a culture for
community 207
Entry 39
The role of the arts in community 211
Entry 40
Culture creators, not just
consumers 215

Entry 41
A culture of creative resistance   221
Entry 42
A community of cultural diversity   227
Recipe
Lamb toshka with Marhaba house salad   231

Section 11
The politics of people power   233
Entry 43
Personal, relational, and structural power   235
Entry 44
Traditional power and transformative people power   241
Entry 45
Subverting dominating institutions   245
Entry 46
Forming alliances to counter the politics of division   249
Recipe
Banana bread   253

Section 12
Endings ...   255
Entry 47
Communities that are connected do better in disaster   257
Entry 48
Energy, food, and water preparation   261
Entry 49
Local work and global connections   265
Entry 50
Active hope and working with despair   269
Entry 51
Celebration!   273
Recipe
Co-op classic choc chip cookies   277

Conclusion   279
References   285

Foreword
A dialogue with practice wisdom
Anthony Kelly

I have been privileged to know all the contributors of this journal. In truth, I have known them not just across a number of years but a number of decades, and I have admired how they have contributed to the ongoing task of building stronger, safer, and more inclusive communities. In some ways, the contributors can be likened to the elders of Indigenous peoples as the carriers of stories and wisdom and as 'elders' of the community development tradition. But the likeness with Indigenous elders is limited because there is little by way of ritual or ceremony that brings together and embeds the breadth of wisdom, decades in the making, of diverse and tested community development practice. That lack of ritual and ceremony is felt not only in bringing together and communicating diverse wisdom but, even more importantly, in its reception. Where are the rituals and ceremonies of the levels of readiness to hear, try, test, shape, and create community development wisdom? My hope is that this journal can be a vehicle that brings together the giving and facilitates the receiving of that practice wisdom. Only the course of time will be the measure of that.

So much community development practice wisdom is commonly communicated in short phrases or gestures, such as 'listen and then listen again' or, in this example, its converse gesture, putting a finger across the lips as a critical reminder that there is too much talk and not enough listening. Practice wisdom is direct but multilayered, with multiple meanings amenable to many situations. We need to appreciate its simplicity and complexity in its one breath, for the richer the wisdom, the more diverse is its importance in context, timing, and meaning. The special gift of this journal, and take note of it, is how often the wisdom is authored/owned and in direct speech – direct speech and not just an abstract thought or concept. Direct speech gives us access to the person. Then, if you can, respond to their words with your own words, not just with a 'what do I think about that' response. Your words, in response to theirs, have the beginnings of a dialogue, and dialogue makes the task of learning much more personal and real, and above all so much easier.

We know well the noise of modern life and feel our fractured attention span as electronic screens occupy greater and greater proportions of our time. The constancy and repetition of so much of our screen life is addictive, and we indiscriminately absorb the good and the bad in both life habits and ideas. Practice wisdom is a combination of the deliberate use of good ideas and good habits, but in the flood of modern data, how do we discern that? Coleridge, that great English poet, reminded us that good ideas are powerful, which is of course their utility, but also the words we use to express these ideas are a beautiful music of the voice. Practitioners who have had the privilege of working through translators have experienced the truth of Coleridge's comment when they hear the beauty of the sounds of the words of wisdom without distraction from the importance of the content. Can a journal give us the space to be open to both?

A journal is a journey, and I wish that all who travel that journey in the company of such dear colleagues travel well, travel safe, and travel with a gentle touch with all that you may encounter.

Anthony Kelly
Co-author of *Participatory Development Practice: Using Traditional and Contemporary Frameworks*
Brisbane/Meanjin
26 April 2025

Acknowledgements

Each of us as authors acknowledges those who matter below, but collectively we acknowledge the following:
- Wendy Pederick from the town of Wagin, Western Australia, a wise woman in her community who is an active citizen and community builder. We are grateful to Wendy for putting aside time to be a reader of the draft manuscript in early 2025, giving us excellent tips to improve the journal.
- Tomo Shimoyukawa from the Sunshine Coast region of Queensland, Australia, was our second reader. Again, we are very grateful for her careful and committed read, and not only the feedback but her courage to give many of the experiments a go.
- Anthony Kelly, now in his 80s and an elder of this practice, has again stepped up and written a foreword. Thank you, Anthony, in this big year for you.
- We are thankful to the following people who tested each recipe and gave helpful feedback: Lara Cooper, PJ Humphreys, Robyn Lawrence, Tina Lathouras, Lisa Price, and Lisa Westoby.
- Fiona Miller, from Jeder Institute, was our creative ally, stepping in to doodle her way into our front cover and section images. Thanks.
- To all the folks from Nundah Community Enterprises Co-operative who generously shared their stories, recipes, and love of sharing food for this journal: you are amazing and thank you.
- You won't see any entries directly written by one of our authors, Gerard Dowling, but he is there through the whole book and is the crafter of most of the experiments. For his light touch throughout, we are all deeply grateful.
- Finally, we acknowledge our faithful publishers at Practical Action Publishing who have been ever responsive, committed to excellence, and have valued our work. A particular thanks to Rosanna Denning and Chloe Callan-Foster.

Peter Westoby

I thank the many people who have invited me into their community and then welcomed me – so many kind, generous, helpful, hospitable, and decent people in local groups, organizations, and neighbourhoods.

I particularly thank the active and committed citizens of Welcome to Maleny, the local refugee support and advocacy group in my neighbourhood that constantly inspires me. They walk the talk.

I also thank all the people who have taught me community building, in words and action. So many. Finally, a deep heartfelt thanks to my partner/wife Rachael Donovan (co-author) for the hundreds of invisible hours put in to make this book happen. I love more and more who and what we are together and separately.

Dave Andrews

My name is Dave, short for David. My parents told me David meant beloved. And I have grown up as a David, feeling loved by my father and mother, then by my wife, my children, and my grandchildren, and then by my many friends. I feel as if my identity is in being loved, and my destiny is being able to love others as I have been loved myself.

I feel like I'm like Obelix, a cartoon character in the Asterix books, who is the protagonist's pal. Like me, Obelix has long hair and a large girth; he is not particularly smart but has prodigious strength. His power is derived from a vat of magic potion that he was fortunate enough to fall into. I have no doubt that any power I have is derived from the vat of magic potion of love, brewed by my tribe, which I was fortunate enough to fall into.

Howard Buckley

There are people who touch your life profoundly, and they support you to get involved and find your place. Lisa, my partner, has been this to me. She has been my friend and co-worker in many of our dabbles with community work, and her influence and care have been enormous for me. She is also mum to our three children, Jessica, Vanessa, and Adam, whose patience with their parents' struggles to be active in their community while being parents cannot be understated. Often, our community involvement meant our children had to 'tag along' or be sidetracked by other agendas. Yet they didn't complain, and now as adults they are involved in building community in their own ways. In contributing to writing this book, I want to acknowledge all the children who have watched and learnt from their parents doing community work. The cycle of hope continues.

Rachael Donovan

To the lands, countries, and ancestors that hold me, heal me, and remind me I belong: thank you for your quiet strength and deep wisdom. To the many people and communities who have shared stories, struggles, and teachings: you have shaped my understanding of what it means to build and be in community. To my beautiful children, Ethan, Daikin, and Isis: you teach me every day what it means to be human, to love deeply, and to stay close to what really matters.

To my husband, Peter: your love, support, and steady presence have helped me stay true to this path. And to all the beings – present and past, human and more-than-human – who guide, challenge, and teach me along the way: I honour your presence, your wisdom, and I give thanks. This journal is a weaving of all you have offered me. I carry your voices in these pages.

ACKNOWLEDGEMENTS

Kirsty Leigh

To my wife and young family: you fill my days with laughter, joy, comfort, and just enough chaos. To my mum and dad, who taught me that hard work and community involvement bring lasting rewards. To my colleague and mentor, Richard, whose boundless compassion and patience inspire me. And to the wonderful people of Nundah Community Enterprises Co-operative, who keep me both on my toes and grounded. I'm so grateful to have shared this remarkable journey with you all.

Gerard Dowling

I'm grateful for all the colleagues I've shared a 'we' moment with. I've learned something silent and somatic from your process skills, every time.

Richard Warner

We labour for much of our lives under the mistaken belief that 'I' am separate from 'you', ignoring the truth that we exist in common. This goes out to the key people in my community. Firstly, Mum and Dad, natural community builders who welcomed the local neighbourhood into the life of our family. My wife, Camilla, and son, Hugo, who are my heart community. Morrie O'Connor, whose work alongside the most disadvantaged has shown me how to 'listen to the people' and support their capacity for collective action. The Community Living Association, Nundah Community Enterprises Co-operative, and Sun Mountain Zen communities who keep me engaged and grounded. Roshis Mervyn and Cecilie Lander, who have taught me over a quarter of a century that the heart of Zen practice is steadfast and caring relationships. Finally, I'd like to thank many friends with disabilities, who helped me learn how to live with a disability and not let it define me.

Community Praxis Co-op and the Nundah Community Enterprise Co-operative (NCEC)

Our collective of authors comes from Community Praxis Co-op and the Nundah Community Enterprise Co-operative (NCEC). We thank both organisations for the ways they have shaped our practice. Community Praxis, through its long-standing community animation work, and NCEC, through its commitment to inclusive, dignified employment. These enduring lessons in relational, participatory community building underpin the spirit of this journal.

Introduction
By Peter Westoby

Why 'community' and why 'now'?

For us as a collective of authors, community has something significant to offer that is fundamental to our hopes for a more just, inclusive, sustainable, and peaceful world. Community foregrounds the many ways 'we' as people connect in meaningful ways, in different places.

In many ways, community signifies connecting to a place, to one another, to becoming 'place-literate', as Canadian author-elder Stephen Jenkinson phrases it (Jenkinson, 2018). Community is a way of thinking about our deep entanglement with one another, a relational approach that reminds us of how we develop a sense of belonging, significance, and solidarity. It helps us understand how we 'make sense' of the world, as we often forget that morality and meaning are a relational process. We learn about how to be in the world – what's right and wrong – through relationships. And relationships are at the heart of community.

Yet community is not the panacea for everything. Community can even be a haunting problem – for example, prioritizing 'some' at the expense of 'others', or using the idea of 'community' to exclude rather than include or build. Community can be a conservative force for maintaining the status quo or a radical force for transformation. The concept of 'community' is often used loosely by many without a clear understanding of its meaning. This workbook will help the reader navigate these kinds of complexities and contradictions, little by little over the time they put aside.

In an era where people are incredibly equipped technologically, are literate about how to buy something instantly, and are hooked into a hyper-capitalist world, there's a deep sense of collective sickness. Due to a lack of purpose and meaning, people are either pulled from or turn away from community at a time when it is most needed.

We hope this workbook can be part of the antidote. A medicine of the social soul. A soothing balm to heal culture – culture that can again animate and orient people towards one another. A way to take action. A pathway to nurture and create community.

Some initial tips about what's helpful

1. Don't assume community just happens. It requires effort and intention. Some people are naturals. You will know people who are natural builders of community in their street and also in the neighbourhood. We all do.

2. Make the building of community more intentional and conscious. Invest.
3. Learn some skills in community building. Most worthwhile things require practice. Nurturing community requires some knowledge, attitudes, and abilities. The provocations in the 51 entries should help you develop or reskill in these areas.
4. The intention behind this conscious and learning practice about community is really about healing our culture. In many ways, our culture is being torn apart by larger social, economic, and political forces. Building community is working against the tide. Allow time for rest as well.
5. Recognize that orienting towards community does not mean neglecting the self. It requires a balance of self–other, of individual–community. Each author of this book deeply values their own quiet space, their solitude, their alone time. We urge you to draw on your spirituality, nurturing an inner life alongside an active outer life. Take care of yourself, and allow time for rest too.
6. While the word 'community' is typically thought of in the context of human relationships, this journal also considers relationships with the more-than-human world, the other beings with whom we, as humans, also share space, the larger environment to which we are intrinsically connected, part of, and dependent on. We will consider how to connect with, nurture, and live in harmony with the larger natural landscape as part of the guided activities and reflections.

With all this in mind, this book is written for

- citizens who are already making things happen in their streets, neighbourhoods, places, and workplaces, who would like a series of prompts and reflections to support a more conscious and intentional 'practice';
- people who'd like to be more active in their streets, neighbourhoods, or workplaces, but aren't sure how to;
- people who feel somewhat isolated and sense that they would like to put a year's effort into building or nurturing community where they live, work, or play.

What does the 'builder' mean?

As a collective, we've grappled with the right word to describe our approach. Some wanted nurturers, others weavers, but we settled on 'builders'. To build community implies discipline, a step-by-step process, and plenty of 'work'. To build is all those things. A wall won't build itself. A builder is needed. And so it is with the community these days. It no longer just happens. Of course, building can also be fun. Perhaps think of it as fun work.

Why is this workbook called a journal?

Peter, one of the authors and editors of this book, loves journals. He's been collecting them for years. When he's travelling, he likes to find a bookshop and buy a journal. It has become a ritual for him, and he has journals from around the world, each enriched with his memories of the place from which it came.

He has also dreamed of owning a shop that sells only journals, accompanied by a cup of tea or coffee.

On that decades-long journey with journals, he noticed the recent tsunami of guided journals available to consumers. Not just blank-page journals for reflection and writing, but journals that guide and prompt. Everything from simple gratitude journals, through to more intentional workshop-like journals, such as Julia Cameron's popular *The Artist's Way* (Cameron, 1992).

However, what he also noticed is that all these guided journals focus on the self: how to be a better individual, a stronger woman, a self-guided powerhouse. Now, as will become clear in this journal, it's nearly impossible to be of service to others in community over the long haul without looking after ourselves, individually and collectively. But he sensed something was out of balance. What if all this 'self stuff' ultimately contributed to a self-oriented culture?

We hope that question hasn't led anyone to discard the book. After all, it's just a question, and questions are good to ask.

Peter began to have conversations with friends, colleagues, and compatriots, and some of those who shared his question have come together as authors of this book.

As authors and community workers, the real dance of life is between self and other, between the individual and the community. And in this book, we're pushing towards the latter. Other. Community.

This is a journal that supports citizens in being more active, intentional, and conscious in building community. It doesn't suggest that citizens aren't already doing this. After all, many communities thrive on people connecting, getting together, supporting one another, forming groups around hobbies, hopes, dreams, and shared experiences, that is, making a community, yet perhaps not intentionally or consciously. The truth is, however, that some communities are not thriving. We hope this journal can support you, in your journey of building thriving communities in small ways.

The basic tools and contents

This journal is a workbook; that is, it's a book to be read over a year, which requires a bit of work, in the sense of reading and reflecting on one of the 51 entries each week (and this introduction for week 1). Each entry includes:

- a key idea or concept;
- a story or two;
- some questions to reflect on;
- an invitation to have a go at something – what we call an 'experiment in practice';
- another invitation to then write some reflections about how the experiment went, and other thoughts or conversations that arise.

You have some space for writing in this journal, but you might want to buy another dedicated journal to allow deeper reflection and to document your experiments.

We suggest setting aside a regular time each week. Make a cup of tea or coffee, or something else you find nourishing. Then, sit in a quiet space and read the story and the accompanying questions. Read it once. Then re-read it. Consider what's being explored: the ideas, the actions.

Then, take time to think about the invitation to an experiment in practice. Mostly, these are small things, such as having a conversation with someone you might not usually talk to. Sometimes they are bigger, such as 'write a letter to your neighbours inviting them around for an afternoon tea', or 'find two other people in your community who share a similar aspiration to you and get together'. Additionally, experiments are guides, not to be done every week necessarily. Be realistic. We're not asking you to do all the experiments, as that would be too much. Some of them are pretty big experiments, and it's okay to be realistic. It is also okay to do this in your own time frame, which may be more (or less) than a year.

Then write about how you intend to conduct your version of that experiment.

Then, later in the week, sit down and reflect on how it went.

Our philosophy of learning is that people learn through a combination of action and reflection. Reflection is key. We all make mistakes, or things don't go as hoped – after all, we can never actually know how someone else will respond to an invitation – so reflection is crucial.

So, do a few things each week – read, reflect on the reading, experiment, reflect on the experiment. We've tried to make things fun and creative wherever possible, as these are important and sometimes forgotten aspects of community building.

Then there's the added cooking opportunity, once a month, to celebrate new connections and nurture the community by cooking up a feast. We offer 12 recipes that have been cooked up by the Nundah Community Enterprises Co-operative (NCEC). We believe food is one of the best ways to connect with others in a relaxed and informal way, which can support community to flourish and grow.

Although this is designed as a weekly journal, we have grouped the provocations into two parts and an interlude, with 12 themes (approximately one per month). For example, this means that if you did one per week, you would spend about a month on a theme and then celebrate with a cook-up before moving on to the next theme. And yet, this journal is a guide. It can be approached in a linear way – from beginning to end, or in a random way as you see fit.

Part 1 is titled *'Orienting, understanding, building, and sustaining'*. We invite you to work through this part systematically, week by week, in the order we have written.

Part 2 is titled *'Pathways of connecting and change'*. This part is organized along the themes of ecology, culture, society, politics, disasters, and 'endings'. We would of course encourage you to read the endings at the end. But the other themes could be read in any order.

The interlude includes four reflections on what's hindering you. We have placed these in the middle of the book, but they can also be read at any time you might feel stuck. Perhaps the wisdom and experiments of this interlude might help you get unstuck.

Within this two-part and interlude structure, we have 12 themes:
1. Orienting ourselves towards community building
2. Understanding community
3. Building purposeful connections
4. Building small groups
5. Sustaining groups
6. What hinders your involvement in community building?
7. Ecological communities
8. Economics as if community matters
9. Community through a social lens
10. Culture and cultural change
11. The politics of people power
12. Endings...

Approaches:

Solo, your household, or a group in the neighbourhood or workplace

There are many ways you could approach your year of community building.
- You could do it alone, making this a solo journey. You will learn about community building through solitary action and reflection.
- You could also do it as a household. A few people from your household or family could follow the suggested rhythm. The process then becomes more of a discussion, with both individual and collective reflection.
- You could get together with some acquaintances or friends in the neighbourhood and do it.
- Or you could do it with a small group of work colleagues (we suggest at least two, because we believe that three people, connected by 'three mutual relationships', is a core building block of community).
- Or you could do it in any other configuration or combination of the above.

Essentially, you can do it alone or with others.

Participating in activities with others has its strengths; this is the power of a group. As is sometimes attributed to Margaret Mead, 'Never doubt that a small group of thoughtful, committed citizens can change the world; indeed, it's the only thing that ever has'[1].

And then there's the enthusiasm generated with others, and of course there's also the accountability. In saying you'll do something out loud to someone else, there's a sense of 'good' pressure to do it! But some love to journey thoughtfully alone, plus right now there might not be someone else to do it with.

Living the question

Fifty-one provocations. Yet the real opus, or alchemical work, is *living the question*. We want you to find your question. It might be something like 'How can I be of service to humanity, or life?' Or it might be as simple and profound as 'How can I contribute to building a more caring, just, and sustainable community in my street, neighbourhood, or workplace?'

As the very first 'worky' thing of this workbook, we ask that you take a few days to think about your question, and then, when it is clear to you, write it in this box.

Your question

What to expect

As you work through this journal, you will hopefully experience moments of joy and enthusiasm. A new kind of conversation. A possible new friend. A new sense of connection to a few folks in your street. Maybe a group forming that wants to do something together.

But there will be harder feelings, or more negative ones. For example, you may feel frustration or annoyance when people fail to reply or follow through on what they said they would do. A new group might fall apart, or life's exhaustion might overwhelm the energy initially generated.

The key point is that community isn't easy – healing culture and reskilling cooperation pushes against the tide. There's no pain-free recovery. But we can make slow, conscious, small steps.

Who are we: our journeys

The seven authors of this book have been involved as 'community builders' for decades, both as active citizens in the streets and neighbourhoods they live in (or have lived in) and as professionals in community development-oriented organizations.

Dave Andrews, his wife Ange, and their family have lived and worked in intentional communities with marginalized groups of people in Australia, Afghanistan, India, and Nepal for over 50 years. Dave and Ange and their friends started Aashiana, Sahara Charitable Trust, and Sharan in India, community organizations working with slum dwellers, sex workers, drug addicts, and people with HIV/AIDS. Dave and Ange have two daughters and four grandchildren, and these days live with one of their daughters, two of their grandchildren, and a half-dozen others in a joint household in West End, where they are part of the Waiters Union. This inner-city community network walks and works alongside First Nations people, refugees, and people with disabilities in Brisbane, Australia. Dave is interested in radical spirituality, intentional community, and the dynamics of personal and social transformation. He is a trainer for Community Praxis Co-op, an elder emeritus of Servants to Asia's Urban Poor, and the author of numerous books and articles.

Howard Buckley lived in the small town of Maleny for over 30 years. He was actively involved in numerous voluntary activities, including contributing to the development of the local neighbourhood centre. He began his journey in community work in the 1980s, honing his skills through voluntary work with young people and refugees in a suburb of Brisbane, and joining with his friends to establish a vocation in community work. For 11 years, he held the part-time role of manager of a youth service in outer Brisbane, which led to many forays into creative community work with young people and their families. Howard recently moved to Caloundra with his partner, Lisa, and is very involved in the lives of his young grandchildren, whom he loves being with. Howard loves bushwalking, camping, the beach, and venturing into wild places.

Rachael Donovan was born and raised in Meanjin/Brisbane and currently lives on Jinibara Country, Maleny, with her husband and co-author, Peter Westoby. Her early life was difficult and fragmented as she moved between different families in state care. Despite this disconnection, she found solace and a deep sense of belonging in the natural world, which has remained a source of strength, wisdom, and love throughout her life. Her years spent in foster care drew her to working with others who experience marginalization or lack of agency and belonging. After years of studying social science, community development, and, later, environmental management at university, she has spent the last two decades working in community development and advocacy roles that facilitate people's voices being heard and included in local action and public policy. Her area of passion lies in the connection between environmental issues and social justice, as well as facilitating healing for both people and the planet. Rachael is also the proud mum of three amazing adult humans and *naani* (grandmother) to one very gorgeous five-year-old grandson.

Gerard Dowling descends from Irish, English, and Scottish ancestors, who journeyed to the colony of Queensland, before there was an official Australia, between 1863 and 1882. Gerard grew up in the remote mining town of Mount Isa, on the lands of the Kalkadoon Nation, playing rugby league and writing poetry. Gerard studied community development at the University of Queensland in his early twenties. He worked as a professional practitioner in various roles in Brisbane for over 30 years, initially learning alongside co-authors Dave Andrews and Peter Westoby in the inner Brisbane suburb of West End, where he raised a young family. In 2019, he retired to care for his ageing mother in her little brick bungalow on Yugambeh land, south of Brisbane, and together they made an intimate and profound journey to the end of her days in her own home. Gerard is currently recovering from mental illness and coming to terms with a diagnosis of adult ADHD neurodiversity at the age of 60. Editing this book marks the first project he has undertaken in two years. Gently. One hour at a time.

Kirsty Leigh grew up around Yarun/Bribie Island/Ningi, where her family were active in building community when the population was small and remote. School holidays were spent exploring the area's diverse ecosystems and witnessing the region's development. This experience was pivotal in her journey, which led her to study sustainable development, combining cafe work with efforts to help restaurants become more sustainable in London, UK. Now Kirsty works at the NCEC using a triple-bottom-line lens to create meaningful work for people with diverse abilities. In this journal, she brings us simple, sustainable recipes to suit a range of occasions. From a wholesome meal to share, to a sweet treat to get you through the tougher section(s) in this journal,

Kirsty's recipes are inspired by popular dishes created and sold at NCEC's hospitality enterprises.

Richard Warner grew up along the Maiwar or Brisbane River. His life was changed when he decided to visit a local institution for people with cerebral palsy – a place few people in his community knew about. This led to adventures with new-found friends as he supported their dreams of leaving the institution's grounds and finding acceptance and inclusion in the broader community. It also led to taking up formal study as a community worker. Little did he know that relationships with people with a disability would be a significant support when he lost his hearing to Ménière's disease in his mid-twenties. Richard now has two cochlear implants and has managed NCEC for 15 years. He has a passion for meditation and has studied Zen Buddhism for 25 years, recently taking on teaching duties in his local sangha.

Peter Westoby lived in the inner Brisbane neighbourhood of West End for 30 years, where he cut his teeth in community building, first as a volunteer and then student, then as a part-time worker. He learned from mentors, such as Dave Andrews, a co-author of this book, and those considered marginalized, such as people living with mental health struggles, those from refugee backgrounds, and, later in life, people experiencing poverty in South Africa, Papua New Guinea, the Philippines, and most recently Nepal. He keeps on learning. Now he lives with Rachael Donovan in Jinibara Country, Maleny, Australia. When not enjoying coffee shops, bookshops, waterholes, and walking trails, he loves working with Community Praxis Co-op, while also enjoying a part-time academic life at Murdoch University in Perth and the University of the Free State in South Africa. He has written over 15 books and published approximately 60 professional journal articles, and is considered a global thought leader in community development.

And our two organizations

The seven of us also work for two organizations. Peter, Gerard, Howard, Rachael, and Dave work for Community Praxis Co-op. This cooperative, established in 1998, has a vision to support peaceful, just, and sustainable communities. One of its contributions to community service is a 20-hour course that we have conducted over 120 times in various locations. Called Building Better Communities, or the Community Animators Training course, we have learned a great deal about how to nurture the kind of relational practices that make community more possible along with effective community action work. This journal offers an opportunity to share the wisdom gained from those courses with many others.

Richard and Kirsty work for the NCEC, which was also established in 1998, creating meaningful and inclusive work opportunities for people who live with intellectual disabilities and mental illness. The Nundah Co-operative, as it is known, has taught us many lessons in community building that are purposefully inclusive of those often left on the edges, disadvantaged, or marginalized by systems of welfare and economics.

Knowing what's ahead and who we are as a collective of authors, now let's begin!

Endnotes
[1] The source is unverified but often attributed to Margaret Mead.

Part 1
Orienting, Understanding, Building, and Sustaining

We invite you to work through this part systematically, month by month, and week by week, in the order we have written.

The sections are ordered as follows:

1. Orienting ourselves towards community building
2. Understanding community
3. Building purposeful connections
4. Building small groups
5. Sustaining groups
6. Interlude: what hinders your involvement in community building?

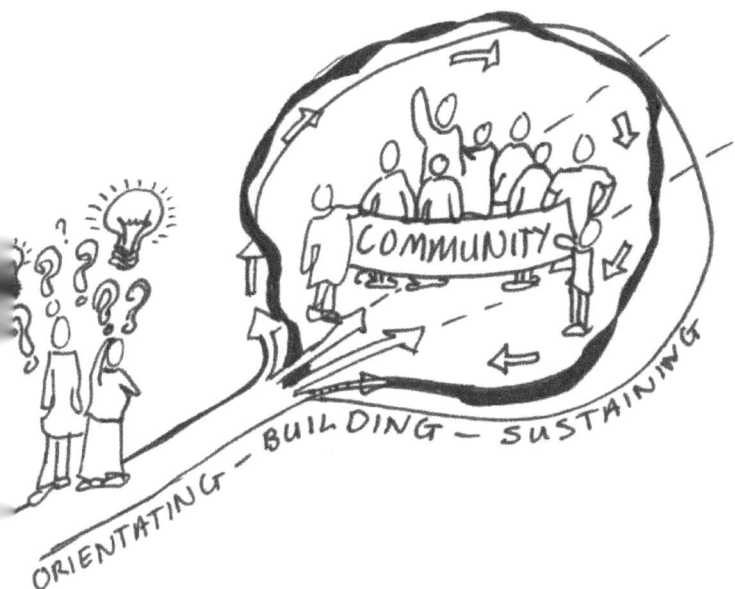

Section 1: Orienting ourselves towards community building

In section 1, we orient ourselves towards a community approach, guided by one of our authors, Peter Westoby.

Peter brings his more than 40 years of experience in community building to orient us towards what we think of as five foundational ideas and practices:

1. **Time, patience, and space**, which remind us that community building does take time, and as such, we need patience.
2. **Experimenting with action** invites us not to worry about getting it right. Building off Gandhi's idea of 'experimenting', Peter invites us to 'have a go'.
3. **Noticing community as an emergent phenomenon** reminds us not to leap into action or activity, but to start by 'noticing' and observing first. Here, we can sense what's already happening in our streets, neighbourhoods, or workplaces, and work *with that*.
4. **Start with what's strong, not with what's wrong.** Dancing with a saying of Dublin-based community development thinker Cormac Russell, we're reminded to start with the strengths of communities, not what they lack.
5. **Relationships matter** is a central principle of community building. This is the essence of what community is: a relationship; therefore, a focus on community building foregrounds these relationships.

To guide our efforts in orienting towards community, this section includes five experiments in practice.

- **Experiment 1. Our relationship with our community** invites us to take a stroll and reflect on what our connection to our community is. Is it just a place? Perhaps a space? Or a base?
- **Experiment 2. Offering a gentle invitation** invites you to introduce an idea thoughtfully into your community.
- **Experiment 3. Seeing your community as if for the very first time** suggests approaching it with a 'beginner's mind' and seeing what you see then.

- **Experiment 4. Noticing what's strong, then shifting it to the foreground** challenges us not to focus on what's wrong, but instead to start with what's strong.
- **Experiment 5. Foregrounding quality in our relationships** asks us to look afresh at our relationships.

This is a crucial section. It orients, frames, and provides some foundational principles and practices. Keep coming back to them. Enjoy!

You can learn more about Peter Westoby at www.peterwestoby.com

Entry 1: Time, patience, and space

By Peter Westoby

As we embark on this year-long journey as community builders, our starting point for the week is to reflect on the nature of time and space in community building.

If you picture a spider weaving a web, one obvious thing is that it takes time for the web to be woven. It's not a case of one moment it's not there, and then the next it is. The web needs to be created, made, or built – it's a process.

Building community – or, as we prefer to think of it, creating the conditions for community to flourish – takes time. After all, at the heart of community is what we sometimes refer to as 'thin trust', that web of social connectivity where we can usually trust a stranger to be helpful, friendly, and civil. And it takes time for this trust to grow in the webs of relationships that make a community. It may also require a step of courage on our part to trust others. The point is that it all takes time, and therefore patience.

Give yourself the gift of time

As we begin, we invite you not to rush to make change. This journal will guide you through a year-long process.

When I moved into the neighbourhood I now live in, I felt an initial impulse to connect with many people and groups, the urgency to get something happening, contribute, and 'make a change'. However, I quickly realized I would become exhausted from being over-connected or over-committed if I went too quickly.

So I decided to give myself a year to meet people, to attend forums, events, and celebrations of a few existing groups, listen to local stories, and read the local newspaper, before I decided to commit myself to *anything*. I wanted to practice that age-old quality of patience and discernment.

I asked myself questions such as 'Where might my energies and skills align with a group or community organization, or an issue that matters to me and others?', 'What is already in place that I can leverage, or might something new be needed?', and 'Who are the people I enjoy being with?'

It took time to work this out.

So, give yourself time. Don't rush this journey in community building.

The space–place–base model of community

As a group of community builders, we also like to apply the wisdom known as 'space–place–base' to make sense of what is happening in the street, neighbourhood, or workplace.

> 'Space' refers to people who simply reside in a locality or come to work to do their job. They don't shop or recreate there, and they don't have friends there. They just come and go from the space.
>
> However, some people *transform* space into 'place'. By this, we mean they learn to love the place. They grow to care about it. They get a sense of belonging from being there. For them, the space has not changed, but their relationship with it has – it's becoming a *place* of connection.
>
> Furthermore, some people go even further. The place becomes their 'base'. They start to take responsibility for it. They not only care, but they also get involved, participate, initiate, and contribute. It energizes the rest of their life and becomes central to who they are and how others perceive them.

Over that first patient year it took me to discern what to get involved in, I was also allowing my relationship with the neighbourhood to transform. Was this just to be a space I lived in, or a place I loved as well? Or was it also a base to get involved in some things?

I gave myself time to discern what my relationship would be!

REFLECTION

- Notice within yourself whether you have a sense of urgency or feel patient about embarking on this community-building journey.
- How might you gift yourself more time to think about the kinds of questions I asked myself?
    - What is already going on that you can connect into, or might something new be needed?
    - Who are the people you enjoy being with?
- If it feels like just a space, what can you do to transform it into a place?
- If it feels like a place, what would you need to do to make it more of a base?
    - Are you ready for that kind of relationship with it?

Experiment 1

Our relationship with our community

Our first experiment gets you out and engaged in a community. When we did our early training more than 40 years ago, it was called 'eyeballing' – a clumsy word, but it conveys the embodied nature of this *reflective* practice.

1. Go for a walk around your neighbourhood or workplace. As you walk, reflect on what your relationship is to your street, neighbourhood, or workplace.
    - o Does it feel like a space, a place, or a base? To what extent?
    - o Have you felt any movement from one to the other over time?
2. When you get back, write a quick poem or a few sentences about what your relationship currently is, and where you would like to take it over the next month or so.
3. Write down the first three thoughts that come into your head in response to this question: 'What does this locality want from you in this year-long process of getting to know it better?'

Entry 2: Experimenting with action

By Peter Westoby

In my early twenties, Dave Andrews, co-author of this book, suggested that I read Gandhi's autobiography. I was a young, enthusiastic community worker, and yet I hardly knew this work had a name. The story of Gandhi captivated me: his journey towards his truths, intentional community building, and aligning the means and ends in social change work, non-violence, and resistance.

But one thing that has stayed with me for decades is the subtitle of the book: *The Story of My Experiments with Truth*.

He never set out to wilfully plan any changes rigidly, whether about his diet, love, community, or social change work. He experimented; that is, he gave something a go, reflected on it, adapted, and kept going.

He was attentive to new possibilities and practicalities without a dogmatic ideology. His ideals were always at the forefront, but his non-ideological commitments enabled him to stay in an experimental mode.

An experimental approach to community building

This journal adopts a similar experimental approach, inviting readers on a year-long journey of community building through a carefully curated series of experiments. The month-by-month and week-to-week stories, reflections, and nudges offer a structure for experimentation.

With this experimental approach, we offer the following suggestions.

1. **Give things a try without worrying too much.** Just try things. If this journal invites you to have a conversation with someone you might not usually talk to, give it a go. Feel into any resistance within you. Notice any frustration within you. Smile to yourself if it doesn't go so well. Celebrate if a new and unusual connection is forged. The point is to give it a try.
2. **Let go of too much planning.** Planning often comes from a 'command and control' perspective. It's infused with the spirit of 'I am going to start this or that project', or 'I plan to speak to my neighbour today', with the idea of 'I will make it happen'. It puts the emphasis on 'I will'. And this comes with its own shadow of possible failure, as 'your will to do something' hits up against problems, or your neighbour is not in the mood to connect today. In contrast, an experimental approach

begins with a few connections, gathers a group of people together, and observes what emerges. It's less wilful. It's still intentional, yet 'lightly held'.
3. **Bring a gentleness to self and others.** This can mean getting used to using a 'tentative' voice in our tone and choice of words. Words like 'suggest' and 'invite'; for example, 'I suggest we gather for a cup of coffee and talk about our ideas', or 'I invite you to sit and share your vision, and I'll share mine'. These gentle words enable experimental energies.
4. **Reflect, learn, and adapt easily.** This experimental approach holds things lightly enough – aspirations, visions, ideas, and agendas – such that we, and those with whom we are with, can reflect on what's working well or not, learn from experience, and adapt appropriately.

The El Salvadoran football club

I recall having a vision in my twenties to form a football (soccer) team with some El Salvadoran refugees I had got to know. I had a vision. But rather than trying to create a club – a daunting idea for one person – I decided to experiment by simply inviting a few people to gather on a Friday afternoon to kick a ball around. A few mates and I invited some people from El Salvador to join us.

The initial six grew to 10, and then 20, and Friday afternoons soon became a highlight for many people. Men and women joined in; some cheered from the sidelines. El Salvadoreans, as newly arrived refugees, and struggling to speak English, were proficient in their fluency of football moves, making them proud and confident.

Eventually, a few of us formed a team and joined a local league, and a couple of years later, a formal El Salvador Football Club was formed. The key point is that, while having a picture of a project in my head, I let go and experimented with smaller things, which eventually grew into the bigger thing and was a lot of fun along the way, and which made more possible as I was enjoying the process rather than being attached to the outcome.

REFLECTION

- Think of a time you have tried to *make* something happen with a strong picture or image of what that is going to be. How did it go – well, or not so well?
- In contrast, think of a time you had an idea, but instead of trying to make it happen, you simply tried a few things out and allowed something to emerge; that is, you experimented.
- Do you think getting things done gradually is a powerful way of working in the world, or a weaker way of getting things done?
- Do you have an idea about what you'd love to do in your street, community, or workplace?
    - o   How could you use an experimental approach to 'land that idea on the ground'?

Experiment 2

Offering a gentle invitation

This is an imaginary experiment in taking an idea to a community. We, the collective authors, all approach this in our own way when exploring an idea.

Start by revisiting your response to the last bullet point in the reflection, above.

1. Go for another walk in your community, with the idea – what you'd love to do – held lightly in the back of your mind. As you walk, pause and then silently invite your community to engage with your idea, and notice what happens in your imagination.
2. As you continue to walk, play with the wording, making it different each time you silently recite your invitation to yourself.
3. Then, play with how you can frame your invitation in ways that make it easier for someone else to join in.
4. Take some time to sit and jot down notes when you get back, reflecting on how to frame an invitation and what else you may have learned.

Entry 3: Noticing community as an emergent phenomenon

By Peter Westoby

Building a community is filled with the energy of action, and each entry in this book invites you to take action. However, one of the key threads that will weave through the whole book is to balance action with observation and reflection, to balance what we sometimes think of as 'intervention' with noticing.

Noticing invites us to hold our ideas and energy back a little, in order to first observe what is *already happening*. It enables us to humbly step back and see what others are already doing. It is to acknowledge that we won't be building a community, because the community is already present. Our aspirations to achieve something usually work best when aligned with what is already happening and building upon that.

A reflection on noticing also invites thinking about an angle of seeing. I often ask students, 'Does a rainbow exist?' In a sense, it does. But of course, not as a thing. You can never go and find a rainbow. A rainbow is an emergent phenomenon that exists under certain conditions – rain, sun, light, a name, knowledge of what it is, and so forth – so that, when you notice a rainbow, you celebrate, aware that it can be gone in an instant.

Noticing community as an emergent phenomenon: a different angle

I then like to ask students to start noticing community in this way, not as a thing (a noun, we might say), but as an emergent phenomenon. The conditions for community include people talking, connecting, gathering, eating, meeting, celebrating, and creating; that is, community is an emerging phenomenon, a verb, coming into being. Being created, or not. Quite a different angle.

We can start by noticing where community is being formed. Where is it being built?

Then, observe the conditions present at that time and place.

We then work with that, carefully joining in and participating ourselves, in ways that take care not to disturb the emergence already happening.

Notice where community is active. Is it on the streets, in a park, at the library, or in a community centre? Where are the hubs that people gather at in your street, neighbourhood, or workplace? What is the spirit of the community? Is it a spirit of complaint or creativity? Is it a spirit of gossip or collaboration?

Once we are confident in what we think we are seeing, it is essential to check in with the people themselves to verify, to ensure we are interpreting correctly.

The discipline of noticing when we are drifting into interpretation

One wisdom about the practice of noticing is to recognize that it always involves two steps. The first is 'seeing' or 'observing' – what we call the raw facts or feelings. You might see two people animatedly talking to each other. You see 'animation'. You might feel a bit of anxiety because it might sound like they're in a combative conversation. This is when we drift to the second step, which is 'interpreting' or 'sense making'. And this is where we can get a great deal wrong.

We often drift into interpreting without realizing it, as the leap from seeing to interpreting occurs very quickly, almost instantly. In this example, interpreting the animated conversation as combative might be accurate, but it could also be incorrect, and it may be more about how we perceive loud, animated talking.

Therefore, it is best to be aware of what is going on around us, as well as within ourselves, and recognize that these two steps are always present. Try to notice, and when interpretations, judgements, or meaning making arise, pause and go back to seeing and sensing again. After all, we don't want to get our interpretations wrong all the time.

One easy way to 'catch' the flip from *observing* to *interpreting* is to be aware of the level of detail you are seeing. If we are looking at a plant, and we describe all its leaves in the same way, we are interpreting. The fact is that each leaf is different. A literal, factual description of what we are actually seeing will describe *each and every* leaf. Facts will be simple, but there will be lots of them.

I first learned to hone my observation skills in a workshop with Sue Davidoff and Allan Kaplan of the Proteus Initiative in South Africa. Allan and Sue asked us each to find a tree or bush in the garden and spend half an hour writing down all the facts we could about it. We all did that and reported back with great excitement about what we had seen. Then they said, 'Do it again'. So we did, coming back astounded by how much more we could see. Then they said, 'Do it again'.

The point is, the more we do this, the better we get at it. Our observational muscles become stronger, our interpretations more thoughtful. It's a rich, humbling journey. Enjoy it.

REFLECTION

Take a moment this week to notice what's going on around you with fresh eyes and ears.
- Where is community already being made?
  - What do you notice about where and how people are connecting and communicating?
  - What kind of spirit or temper appears to be present – a spirit of complaint or creativity, or something else?
- How can you begin participating in this emerging community?
- What do you notice about yourself this week as a noticing person?
  - Do you leap quickly to interpretation and meaning making, or can you pause on that easily, and see only what is actually happening?

Experiment 3

Seeing your community as if for the very first time

This week's practice is to apply the wisdom gained from above as you continue to observe and reflect on your community.

1. Go for a walk in your neighbourhood or workplace, observing where you see community coming into being as an emerging phenomenon.
2. When you return, sit down and write up each observation you have made.
3. Then make two columns. Close your eyes and remember what you actually saw and, for *each* observation, write a list of the facts as cleanly as you can in one column. Then, as you become aware of them, write your interpretations in a separate list in the other column.
4. You may end up with lists that do not give as much meaning as your original observations in step 2. However, you will have honed your ability to notice *what actually is*.

Entry 4: Start with what's strong, not with what's wrong

By Peter Westoby

When we notice the world, we unconsciously foreground and background certain things. We often don't even know we're doing it. For example, only this morning, as I noticed my garden and home, all I could see were the wild weeds and stuff that needed fixing. This is what my mind foregrounded. I backgrounded the beautiful flowers and fecundity of life. I backgrounded the parts of our home we've fixed up in recent weeks.

In noticing what is going on in the community, we can often unconsciously do the same. For example, most people tend to foreground all the problems and challenges. And of course, there are plenty. There are many social problems in our neighbourhoods, from homelessness, to waste, to youth suicide or loneliness. I could go on. There are numerous urban-planning problems, including footpaths that are either in decay or not connected, as well as a lack of designed hubs for connectivity. Most of our communities are car-centred, making walking or cycling dangerous.

But instead of focusing on these problems, we could also shift our noticing to what's working well. We feel that, in building community, it's better to 'start with what's strong, not with what's wrong'. It's actually a saying coined by a tradition of community building called assets-based community development, and particularly by a Dublin-based colleague of ours, Cormac Russell.

Switching our noticing to what's working invites more of what's strong in our streets, communities, and workplaces. Shifting our gaze – for a while anyway, because we are not going to deny the challenges and problems – so we can see afresh. Some would say it's an act of respect for what actually is – that 're-spect' is 're-seeing'.

A focus on what's working sustains motivation

One of the key lessons from an asset-oriented approach to community building is that it is easier to sustain motivation and energy when we maintain a focus on what is working well, even when collaborating with others to tackle what is challenging. Plus, it's best to build on what's going well anyway.

For example, if we decide to tackle the challenge of social isolation in our community, it's best not to start by gathering all the lonely people. A better approach is to notice where connections are already being made, where people are already gathering, so they're not isolated and less at risk of loneliness.

From there, we can collaborate with others to invite more isolated individuals into these spaces of connectivity through their existing natural networks. We might ask three people who are already coming regularly if they each know someone who would benefit from attending, and invite them, ensuring there are others who will make them welcome when they tentatively join. If there is a particular person we are concerned about, we ask who already has a connection in their world, so the invitation itself comes from a place of a stronger, rather than weaker or absent, existing relationship. The point is, our starting place is 'what's strong'.

Focusing on what's wrong can also lead us down false paths. For example, if a community is focused on crime, community members can often assume that the solution is more police. It's the equivalent of noticing people are getting sicker and sicker in our society, so the solution becomes more hospital beds. Instead, focusing on what's strong for both these issues invites thinking about the role of community connectedness in reducing both crime and illness. From a community-building perspective, health and safety are outcomes of connected and active citizens. And there is plenty of evidence that shows this to be true.

Focusing on learning, through all the difficulties

For a number of years, I have been involved in supporting families whose children have life-limiting illnesses and profound disabilities. On one occasion, we sat in a circle and shared stories of these lived experiences. Initially, there was a focus on the profound and real pain, tussles with ineffective and unresponsive bureaucracy, and annoyances with people in the community who were careless towards those with a disability.

However, at a certain point in the conversation, I inquired about the skills and practices people had developed despite all those difficulties. Pretty quickly, people were focusing on all that they'd learned: the skills of assertiveness, when to say no to bureaucrats who were not listening, and how to find and connect with those who were helpful. The energy in the room shifted as the focus of attentiveness shifted to what they were strong at and what they knew, rather than just the problems. The conversation shifted to real possibilities as opposed to all the barriers.

REFLECTION

- When you think of your street, neighbourhood, or workplace, do you tend to focus on what's wrong or what's strong?
    - Not denying any of the real problems, think about what's strong in your community and how you might build on that.
- How might what's strong already connect to what's wrong in a creative way?
    - For example, what spaces and places are there where people connect and create a sense of belonging, and how can those who are isolated and lonely be linked to those spaces and places?
- Consider an issue that really bugs you. How might shifting to what's strong unlock a more creative relationship with that issue, and new ideas for moving forwards on it?

Experiment 4

Noticing what's strong, then shifting it to the foreground

This week, your practice challenge is to 're-spect' your community, and to shift what's strong to the foreground of your seeing.

1. Make a note of the things that you notice that are 'wrong', the problems and issues in your community. Then make a note of all the things that are 'strong'.
2. Review the two sets of noticings. How does each set feel to read?
3. Now tear up those notes and get a new piece of paper.
4. You may want to use a little bit of creativity (colour, layout, style of lettering, etc.) to express all the things that are strong in your community.
5. Stick it on your wall. Then stick another empty piece of paper beside it, to capture all the other things you notice that are strong in your community over the coming days.

Entry 5: Relationships matter

By Peter Westoby

As we come to the end of this first orienting theme, look back over previous weeks: time and patience, an experimental approach, noticing, and the last one, 'start with what's strong, not what's wrong'. Each is a key signpost to return to as you progress this year of journaling about your community-building intentions and efforts. You might even like to review your notes now.

Certainly, return to these entries as often as feels right. If you're feeling frustrated at a lack of so-called progress, recall the writing and reflections about patience and time. If something has not gone as planned, reconsider the experimental approach and what can be learned from it. If you're feeling too busy, or manic, or wilful, or depressed, pause and spend time noticing. If you're feeling disheartened, and the list of problems is getting longer, reorient yourself towards what's working well in your street, neighbourhood, or workplace.

However, we now turn to a final orienting theme for our journey: the fact that, in all of this, *relationships matter most*.

Those who love people build community

Sometimes in our community-building training, we ask people to meditate on the words of Dietrich Bonhoeffer:

> The person who loves their dream of community will destroy community, but the person who loves those around them will create community. (Bonhoeffer, 1954: 35)

In other words, those who love community destroy it, and those who love people build community.

To love people is to love being in relationships with people, whether that's a casual yarn with a stranger at a coffee shop, or a gentle conversation with the librarian, through to the deeper connection forged through a regular reading group encounter. The point is that, sometimes, on a journey of community building, it may be best to refocus simply on building relationships, which usually leads to the emergence of a community. Remember the idea of community as a verb, emerging. As we relate to one another in ways that build trust, we are creating community.

Of course, there are different kinds of relationships, ranging from casual to deeply significant. All are crucial for community: friends and those you just want to be friendly with; those you see as allies, comrades, or colleagues in a group venture; and those you just want to say hello to over the garden fence.

Four reasons relationships really matter for community

We suggest that relationships matter for several reasons. First, relationships are what make the web, which is crucial for community. It's the web of relationships that enables a community to function. I need something; in a relationship with you, I can get that something. Or you can ask me for something.

Second, relationships are what build trust. And trust is the glue that holds a community together. It's as we relate to people and hear their stories that our own false images or judgements fall away. As the saying goes, 'it's hard to hate someone whose story you know'. As we build relationships, we become more open to people, and trust is gradually established. As people follow through on what they agree to do, so trust is built. As we hear people say good things about others and assume they might speak positively about us to others also, trust is built. As we reach out to people, and then they reach out to us, so trust is built. Trust then acts as a living glue, keeping the web alive. And when trust is alive, all sorts of things become easier, like stronger economies, lower crime rates, and better health. We will explore these topics in the coming weeks. Conversely, if trust starts to erode – due to gossip, or lies being spread, or unresolved conflicts – relationships will start to collapse, undermining the community's capability to do good things together.

Third, people respond in solidarity and support due to their relationships. Our years of experience suggest that people rarely attend an event unless personally invited or unless it features a highly relevant topic or a notable speaker. So, if down the track in this community-building journey you want to gather people around an issue, concern, or dream, they are most likely to come along because you have a relationship with them. Or the person you invite has relationships with others, whom they also invite. The web of relationships is what makes things happen in a community.

Fourth, there are different types of relationships. And we'd like to distinguish between two key types. These are 'non-transactional' and 'transactional' relationships. The latter are relationships where people are paid to be in someone's life. As such, someone might feel like they have a lot of relationships, but upon reflection, see that they're mostly transactional, for example, a social worker, a visit to the doctor, or a friendly librarian or barista. These are important. But non-transactional relationships are the real glue. They're characterized by mutuality, reciprocity, and care. They might not always *feel* like that, because most relationships can go through difficult times. But, generally, they are.

REFLECTION

- When you think of relationships in the context of your street, neighbourhood, or workplace, what comes to mind?
    - Is it a positive thought, or not so positive?
    - Are the relationships hard-going or easy-going?
- Consider the Bonhoeffer quote above. How does it resonate with you?
- Consider your relationships through the lens of both transactional and non-transactional relationships. No judgements, just noticing.
    - Do you have enough relationships in your life that can be characterized as mutual, reciprocal, and filled with care?

Experiment 5

Foregrounding quality in our relationships

This experiment prompts us to reexamine our relationships.

1. In your imagination, scan through your existing relationships within the community you intend to build. Identify three that have potential for growth in terms of reciprocity, mutuality, and care.
2. For this week, simply hold them in the foreground of your active imagination, every day.
    - Do you notice any changes in the way you regard these people?
    - Do you notice any changes in the ways they relate to you?
3. Then, intentionally build qualities of trust, mutuality, reciprocity, and care into those relationships.
    - Set an intention.
    - Reach out to check in on these people.
    - Ask them to check in on you.
    - Offer to do something caring (i.e. drop in with a meal or take them for coffee).
4. Check in over the month. What has changed for you?
    - Has there been an opportunity to chat with the people you identified about what they are experiencing in terms of the quality of the relationship between you?
    - If not, look for an opportunity when it feels appropriate.
    - What might you need to experiment with next?

Recipe
Banana and macadamia granola
Kirsty Leigh

Vegan; gluten free if you get the right rolled oats.
Prep time: 20 minutes. | **Cooking time:** 1–1.5 hours.
20-30 servings

We serve this crunchy, not-too-sweet granola (based on Minimalist Baker's (n.d) recipe) on yoghurt with fresh fruit. It's so tasty that people request to buy it by the bagful! Many an afternoon, I would catch the Nundah Co-operative Coordinator gathering a handful at 3pm when others had gone for the day (you know, just to get himself through until home time). It's super satisfying with your favourite milk. If you can bear to share, it makes a lovely homemade gift: simply add a ribbon around the jar. Voila!

INGREDIENTS

- 3 cups (300 g) of rolled oats
- ¾ cup (110 g) of almonds
- ½ cup (75 g) of macadamias
- 2 tablespoons of raw sugar
- ½ teaspoon of sea salt
- ½ tablespoon of cinnamon
- 1 tablespoon of flaxseed
- ¼ cup (60 ml) of coconut oil
- ⅓ cup (80 ml) of maple syrup
- 1 teaspoon of vanilla bean paste
- 1 medium ripe banana, mashed well

METHOD

1. Preheat the oven to 130°C/250°F/gas mark 1/2.
2. Mix the oats, almonds, macadamias, sugar, salt, cinnamon, and flaxseed together in a large bowl.
3. In a small saucepan, over a medium–low heat, warm the coconut oil, maple syrup, and vanilla bean paste until liquid.
4. Remove from the heat and whisk in the mashed banana until well combined.
5. Pour the liquid over the dry ingredients and mix well.
6. Spread the mixture evenly in a thin layer on a large baking tray (or two) and bake for 1 hour or more, checking every 20 minutes or so, until golden brown. Stir it once during baking. Be sure to watch it carefully as it can brown suddenly.

Stir and allow to cool before transferring to a jar to store for up to a month.

Section 2: Understanding community

In this section, we are introduced to Rachael Donovan, whose experience as a young adult transitioning out of state care shaped her quest for community in both her professional and personal life.

Rachael invites us to consider and explore:

1. **What is this 'community' thing, anyway?** This looks at what we mean when we say 'community', in terms of the ways it is described by some thoughtful authors in the literature on theory and practice, but, more importantly, as an experience that resonates with our values, and informs and motivates our ongoing engagement with community.
2. **Vision and values for community** describes the kinds of vision and values that make a difference to community, and the importance of connecting with and building community with others who share our values and who can become our comrades and allies.
3. **Community as social capital** looks at investing in social capital to establish strong networks that support our efforts and provide opportunities to connect resources with needs in our broader communities.
4. **The dark side of community** explores how 'community' can be harmful when it is used to wield power, enforce exclusion, or enact injustice.

Over the next few weeks, we will map a series of experiments that we hope will engage you with new ways of understanding community, through the lens of your own experiences.

- **Experiment 6. Reflecting on a powerful, formative experience of community** prompts you to engage with and reflect on a story from your own experience that resonates with your values and informs and motivates your current engagement with your community.
- **Experiment 7. Identifying the existing values in your community** invites you into a creative and critical examination of your own values and those you encounter in your wider community.
- **Experiment 8. Investing in your own social capital** challenges you to identify your own social capital and then develop a plan to strengthen your networks.

- **Experiment 9. Initiating a reflective dialogue** to get insight into others' experiences of the dark side of community is the first time we're asking you to bring others into the conversation – whether that's by gathering a small group or having a casual chat with one or two people. Your aim is to guide a reflective discussion about how your broader community collectively responded to the COVID pandemic. Consider what their insights reveal about the 'dark side' of community in your local context.

We hope these reflections and experiments get you engaged with the reality of what 'community' is, what it can become (as an emergent phenomenon), and the dark side it can easily skew into – in your own thinking, and in the wider community you are choosing to engage with.

Entry 6: What is this 'community' thing, anyway?

By Rachael Donovan

Before we discuss the building of community (or creating the conditions for community to emerge), it is helpful to first explore what we mean by 'community'.

Community is a word that everyone knows and uses, but it means different things to different people.

This week, we invite you to first explore what community means to you, not just as an idea, but through your personal experience.

Some helpful descriptions of community

Other writers and thinkers have framed the idea of community in various ways. Here are a few examples that provide a grounding for the theory and practice we explore in this journal.

- **Robert Putnam**, an American political scientist, views community as 'social capital', emphasizing the importance of networks, trust, and reciprocity in building social connections. He argues that strong social capital is essential for the functioning of democratic societies. We will refer to Putman's work at other times in this journal (Putnam, 2000).

- **Peter Block** is an author who defines community as a place where people feel a sense of belonging, have a voice in decision-making, and work together to create a better future. He emphasizes the importance of building relationships and fostering a sense of accountability within communities (Block, 2008).

- **M. Scott Peck** is a psychiatrist and author who describes community as a group of individuals who come together for a common purpose, share values, and support one another in their personal growth and development. He highlights the transformative power of community in promoting individual and collective well-being (Peck, 1987).

- **bell hooks** is a cultural critic and feminist scholar who discusses the importance of intersectionality and inclusivity in defining community. She argues that true community involves recognizing and addressing power dynamics, challenging systems of oppression, and creating spaces where all voices are heard and valued (hooks, 2003).

As you can see from this small sample, there are many different ways of viewing community. In our experience, the more rigorous ways usually include some overlapping focus on connection, trust, belonging, equity, and inclusivity.

Our own experience of community

This week, we invite you to reflect on your definition and story of community.

One of my strongest and most powerful experiences of community was as a 17-year-old. I was living in foster care and had spent many years feeling isolated, alone, and uncared for. Most of the people in my life were paid to be there in some capacity – those transactional relationships mentioned last month.

Fortunately, this sense of isolation began to change when I was connected to the CREATE Foundation, a community organization that supports young people in out-of-home care to connect with each other, build skills and confidence, and have a voice in changing the foster care system.

We would go away to camps, not only having fun, but also sharing and hearing about each other's experiences and stories. *I felt connected*. I participated in a 'young consultant' training programme that helped build my skills and confidence and helped me understand the broader out-of-home care system. *I felt valued*. I was supported to have a voice at conferences and in meetings with government ministers to improve the foster care system. *My voice mattered*.

Through my time at CREATE, I found a deep sense of belonging and a strong sense of community for the first time in my life. Thus, community came to mean *connection and belonging* to me. It has become a place of inclusion, where all voices matter and are valued, particularly those that are marginalized or silenced.

Through this powerful experience of community, inclusion, and connection, I developed enough confidence, support, and self-belief to move towards some of my own life goals, things that I previously thought were impossible. I finished school, enrolled in university, and found my voice in the world. It took time, and the journey wasn't without setbacks, but being part of a community where I mattered and belonged in meaningful ways transformed my life and helped me find my sense of self.

It just goes to show that community, when strong, is a powerful force for transformation and change.

REFLECTION

- When you think of community, what does it mean to you?
- What are the values that are important to you in community?
- Reflecting on the four descriptions of community from the literature above, who do you resonate with most?
- Are there elements that don't feel aligned for you?

Experiment 6

Reflecting on a powerful, formative experience of community

In this experiment, we are looking for a story from your own experience that resonates with your values and informs and motivates your engagement with community.

1. Think of a powerful personal experience of community. It can be recent or from your earlier years.
    o   We are not defining community. It's an experience that feels like community to you.
2. Share this story with a friend or someone in your community builders' group.
    o   Ask them to share with you the keywords they heard you use to describe it as an experience of community.
    o   For example, you might say something like 'it's the first time I felt safe', and the keyword would be 'safe', or it might be 'I finally felt like I belonged', and the keyword would be 'belonged'.
    o   These keywords indicate some of the values and themes that *they see* in your story.
3. Afterwards, find a quiet space and time to write your own description of the kind of experience of community that *you want to have more of*, and that *you want to share with other people*.

Entry 7: Vision and values for community

By Rachael Donovan

Values are high-order beliefs that guide what matters. They may be conscious or unconscious, and they guide our decisions, behaviours, and attitudes.

Like personal values, each community – or group within a community – has a slightly different flavour in terms of what it values. Shared values and vision are what make collective work meaningful, easier, and more effective. It can be challenging when you find yourself in a group or community that holds values that don't align with your own, particularly when it comes to working together for change.

Shared values make our work meaningful

I found myself in this situation in 2010. I had just finished my master's degree in community development and was feeling both frustrated and isolated in my broader community. The lack of cultural diversity and the strong focus on individualism and consumer culture felt out of alignment with my values. I craved diversity and collective ways of being together. I felt like an outsider.

To address this challenge, I became a Couchsurfing (n.d.) host and invited travellers from around the world to stay with me as they explored the region. They would stay anything from a few days to a few weeks, and we would share food, stories, and life journeys. It was a beautiful, rich way of learning and connecting for myself and my family. It allowed me to expand (and challenge!) my thinking and be part of a reciprocal gift economy.

I loved it, but it wasn't enough, and I was becoming increasingly frustrated and isolated. Life eventually took me to India where I spent five years supporting local community work and immersed in a very different culture. I became alive in new ways during that time, as it felt much more aligned to my values, spirituality, and sense of community and belonging.

It took me a long time to find that in Australia, but I eventually discovered that I have the power to build and support community in my own life, wherever I am.

When I moved to Maleny five years ago, I encountered a town rich in community spirit but also marked by divisions. The town is home to many communities: the original farming community, an artistic and alternative crowd, and a newer 'green change' group drawn to the area's scenic beauty. These groups often have different interests and values, which can lead to conflict.

Connecting with others who share our vision and values

As I reflected on what mattered most to me, I slowly connected with others who shared my values. I joined the local Landcare group, became connected with the neighbourhood centre, and regularly visited the Buddhist centre, forming connections with people who resonate with many of my values. I came to understand that I might never find a single community that fully aligns with my values, but I could build meaningful relationships with various people and groups.

Values are important both individually and in our communities. Individually, they help us feel a sense of belonging, trust, and connection. In any community, values help guide our priorities and collective actions; that is, the vision for a community is a way of being and acting among groups of people who share similar values. It's rare that a whole street, neighbourhood, or workplace can agree on values and a vision for all. But some groups do it, and together they tip the scales in certain directions of action.

For example, if environmental sustainability is a core value (as it is for me), a group's vision might focus on becoming a carbon-neutral region. If innovation and education are valued, the vision might aim for a robust economy driven by technology and knowledge-based industries. If resilience and adaptability are valued, the vision might include plans for disaster preparedness and recovery.

Thus, just like personal values, community values guide the priorities and vision of the community. Yet if the values aren't explicit, they can operate unconsciously or in unhelpful ways.

In our work delivering Building Better Communities courses to over 100 places in Queensland, Community Praxis Co-op has learned a few things about the values that make groups robust and healthy. These include:

1. safety;
2. acceptance;
3. respect;
4. inclusivity;
5. involvement; and
6. justice (Andrews, 1996).

Over the years, we've learned that these values support pathways for addressing challenges, fostering resilience, nurturing a sense of collective responsibility, and building a shared vision of well-being for all community members. Of course, in your community, there might be different priorities, and values can change over time or seasons, but these six values have generally stood the test of time for us.

ENTRY 7: VISION AND VALUES FOR COMMUNITY

REFLECTION

- Do your values align with the values of some in your community?
- If not, are there spaces or groups that might be more aligned?
- What is your vision for your community?
    - For example, is it to create a safe space where people feel connected, included, and welcomed?
- How can you dedicate your time to this in your daily life, in both small and larger ways, by joining with others who share a similar vision?

Experiment 7

Identifying the existing values in your community

This week's experiment in practice will engage you in a creative and critical examination of your own values and those you encounter in your wider community.

1. Draw a picture that represents your vision of a healthy community.
    - Identify the values implicit in your picture.
    - Are some of these values present in your community?
2. Now try to more explicitly identify the values in your community, that is, find out what your community prioritizes.
    - You may need to do some research to learn about the history, culture, demographics, needs, challenges, and achievements of your community.
    - You could also ask various community members to gauge the core community values, and/or you might identify where there are some clashes of core values.
3. Reflect on and respond to these questions:
    - How does your community define itself, or is it a case of different groups defining themselves differently?
4. Reflect on the most significant value-related issues and opportunities your community is facing. Jot down your thoughts.

Entry 8: Community as social capital

By Rachael Donovan

Strong social networks and healthy relationships are the cornerstones of community. Relationships of care, mutuality, and reciprocity are what make communities thrive. The stronger these networks are, the more robust and healthier our communities will be.

As mentioned in entry 6, 'social capital' is a term coined by Robert Putnam, referring to the resources, benefits, and opportunities that arise from reciprocal relationships within our communities (Putnam, 2000).

Bonding, bridging, and linking

Putnam describes how different kinds of relationships – bonding, bridging, and linking – come together in a thriving, well-connected, healthy community.

'Bonding social capital' refers to close relationships with people who share similar identities, backgrounds, interests, or experiences. These include friendships, family networks, ethnic communities, or religious groups. Essentially, they are the people we enjoy spending time with because they are like us.

On the other hand, 'bridging social capital' fosters connections across diverse groups from different backgrounds, cultures, or social identities. While it is easier to develop relationships with people who are like us, bridging relationships diversify our networks and can help us develop empathy, understanding, and appreciation for different perspectives and experiences. Building bridging relationships is more challenging when they involve people who are different from us, and they will likely challenge us in some way; this is often a good thing.

'Linking social capital' refers to the connections formed between individuals and groups at different levels of power or authority, such as between people and institutions, organizations, or government agencies. These linkages facilitate access to resources, information, and opportunities that may be controlled by those with more power.

We've probably all experienced the benefits of social capital, and usually the strength of our networks becomes apparent when we have a need that we can't meet or we're faced with an unexpected crisis. At such times, we learn how our relationships or networks can link resources to need (Westoby and Dowling, 2013).

How social capital can link resources to need

One of the women I work with shared a very personal and difficult story that highlights the importance of social capital. A few years ago, she was forced to flee her home with her children due to domestic violence. Being new to the area, she had very few connections and relationships and therefore had no networks to turn to for shelter or support.

She said, 'Many pieces of the puzzle were missing', such as housing, food, support, and other essential resources to help her during this time of desperate need.

Whereas others may be able to turn to family or friends in times of crisis or know which service to connect to for emergency shelter or food, her networks and social capital were limited (i.e. the 'puzzle pieces', as she called it), and she ended up living on the streets. During her time sleeping rough, she slowly built connections of support with other 'rough sleepers' (both bonding and bridging relationships), services, local organizations, and people in positions of power (linking relationships) that helped her through this crisis.

Her growing social capital extended beyond human support during this time, and she tapped into an intimate kind of 'ecological social capital', as the land where she slept became a space of solace, support, and belonging. She told me that she developed relationships with many other species, including a beautiful one with an emu that visited her camp, which offered comfort during this very difficult time.

This story highlights the importance of bonding, bridging, linking, and ecological networks in enabling greater access to resources, information, and support within communities.

REFLECTION

- Take some time to reflect on your own bonding, bridging, linking, and ecological networks.
    o Do they feel strong?
    o Which area is the least developed?
    o How could you consciously develop stronger networks in this area?
- How can you foster stronger bridging relationships?
    o What might be the benefit both personally and in your community?
- What is the risk to individuals and communities if social capital is not strong?

Experiment 8

Investing in your own social capital

This experiment challenges you to identify your own bonding, bridging, linking, and ecological social capital, and then develop a plan to strategically invest in strengthening your networks, enabling you to tap into the four types of social capital that are identified above.

1. Consider times in your life where social capital has in some way enabled your needs to be met with resources, or you yourself have been a resource for someone in need.
   - Identify how your own
     o bonding
     o bridging
     o linking and
     o ecological
   social capital was engaged to meet that need.
2. Reflect on your ancient ancestors and their relationships with the natural world.
     o Do you consider your relationships to the natural world and other species as an important part of your community connections?
     o How could you deepen these connections, and how might this strengthen your social capital?
3. Sketch a plan for starting to strengthen your networks.
     o You want to have networks that bring you within easy reach of bonding, bridging, linking, and ecological social capital, so that next time you need resources, you can access them.

Entry 9: The dark side of community

By Rachael Donovan

Having reflected on your story, vision, and values of community, as well as the importance of social capital as a network of relationships, you can probably now see that community offers a beautiful space of care, belonging, and connection.

Yet, throughout history, 'community' has also been used dangerously, to wield power, exclusion, violence, or injustice. If a sense of justice isn't at the core, community can be easily used to create such harm.

This entry helps us bring greater awareness to the dangerous aspects of community, so we can avoid doing harm. We can experience these harmful aspects individually, within neighbourhoods, and across nations, as explored below.

Individually: a tension between our individuality and community

We all want to be free to be ourselves and feel the deep sense of connection and belonging that comes from being part of a community. To achieve this, we must continually navigate the tension between who we aspire to be and what the world expects us to be.

While the *unity* part of comm*unity* can make us feel good, it also comes with a pressure to conform, particularly for those of us who don't fit within the cultural mainstream. This can lead to suppressing parts of ourselves to fit in or risk being excluded if we fail to do so.

Neighbourhoods: a tension between our backyard and the greater good

All forms of togetherness inherently imply some form of exclusion. Community is no exception. Neighbourhoods might foster unity among 'insiders', but this unity can come at the cost of 'outsiders' who may face alienation or displacement.

The phenomenon known as 'not in my backyard' (NIMBY) brings this paradox to life in a tangible way. NIMBY occurs when residents oppose developments – such as waste facilities, housing projects, or industrial sites – not necessarily because they object to the existence of these facilities, but because they don't want them near their own homes.

People may passionately advocate for changes or protections that benefit their own area while ignoring or even undermining the needs of neighbouring communities. When one neighbourhood mobilizes against a waste facility, for instance, it might lead to the displacement of that facility to a less vocal, less affluent, or less organized community nearby.

Nationally: a tension between identity and violence

At a national level, we can see the potential for the greatest harm in the name of community. At this level, community identity can be used to justify actions that propagate violence.

Nationalism, as an expression of national community, for example, can bring people together with a shared sense of pride; however, historically, it has also been used to justify exclusionary policies or the invasion of other nations. Many wars were started in the name of nationalism. That is why, at Community Praxis Co-op, our motto is 'peaceful, just, and sustainable communities'. We advocate that the strong values of peace, justice, and sustainability must be guiding principles in community work, to ensure that harmful actions are not taken in the name of 'community'.

The danger of community in times of crisis

The COVID pandemic offered a more recent example of both the beauty and the dark side of community. As humanity faced this historic event, a strong sense of solidarity emerged in some places, particularly in neighbourhoods where people supported one another with shopping and other necessities.

However, as the pandemic evolved, the shadow and dark side of community also surfaced, bringing about intense divisions and polarizations. Controversial issues such as lockdowns, vaccination mandates, and mask wearing became flashpoints for disagreement, with polarized views leading to fractured relationships among friends and family. What was meant to be a shared effort to combat the virus transformed into a battleground of differing beliefs, resulting in exclusion and alienation even within close-knit circles.

At the community level, these divisions manifested as physical and social barriers. People were excluded from spaces or activities based on mask-wearing habits or vaccination status, creating an 'in-group' and 'out-group' mentality. Some neighbourhoods or communities established measures to control entry based on health protocols, leading to heightened scrutiny and mistrust of outsiders. This created visible boundaries within communities that were once more open, amplifying a sense of separation.

On a larger scale, entire cities and regions faced extended lockdowns and travel restrictions. Nationally and internationally, borders were closed, sometimes even to their own citizens, reflecting how nations mobilized to protect their own populations at the expense of open exchange and movement. This shadow of community – its tendency to protect insiders at the cost of excluding or even demonizing outsiders – emerged as the fear of external threats increased.

ENTRY 9: THE DARK SIDE OF COMMUNITY

REFLECTION

- Have you ever felt excluded or marginalized in a community (whether that be a neighbourhood, workplace, or other community group) because of who you are, what you believe, or where you come from?
    - How has that experience shaped your view of community?
- Have you witnessed or participated in actions within your community that might have led to someone feeling judged and/or left out?
    - How did that make you feel, and what did you learn from it?
- Reflecting on the COVID pandemic, how did you or your community react to people with different views to yours in terms of the health response?
- How can you be more mindful of these dangers in your own life and community, and what are a few things you can do to mitigate them?

Experiment 9

Initiating a reflective dialogue to get insight into others' experiences of the dark side of community

This is the first time we have put an experiment to you that asks you to convene a group. If that's a step too far for you for now, please just have a casual conversation with a couple of people. Either way, your job is to steer the discussion to reflect on how you collectively handled the COVID pandemic. For this to work, you will need to communicate genuine curiosity when initiating the discussion and focus on listening attentively to what people are saying.

1. Convene a small group of people (or have a casual chat with a few people) in your street, neighbourhood, or workplace and reflect together on how your community handled COVID.
2. Discuss the ways the idea and language of community were mobilized for either inclusion and exclusion – or both.
3. Write or draw your reflections on what happened and how you feel about what happened.
4. What could be learned from this historical experience that could be remembered for any future disaster events?

Recipe
Aleppo chicken and rice

Gluten free.

Prep time: 30–40 minutes and overnight marinade. **Cooking time:** 1 hour. Serves 6.

People come back again and again for this saucy chicken and rice dish. The original recipe was brought to us by a Syrian refugee. The toppings give it an edge that not only looks great but takes it to the next level with crunch, spice, and a sweet chewiness.

Over the years, our chef's, including apprentice Syahmie, experimented with the content, and we feel that this one is worth sharing. We met Syahmie, known to us as Sam, at an event we catered at a local alternative school. They were a shy person with a preference for being busy in the kitchen rather than attending their school graduation. After doing a few shifts at our soccer canteen, we offered Sam a full-time apprenticeship at our new Marhaba Cafe. Sam spent three years in an orphanage, as their single mum couldn't properly care for them, and where they suffered a string of abuse. 'You name the abuse, I had it', said Sam. At the age of seven, Sam started cooking, which was the beginning of a career working in kitchens.

Sam eventually made their way to Australia and, at 13, found themselves working at their father's kebab shop whenever Sam wasn't at school. But things at home weren't good, so as soon as it was possible, Sam went to the police and 'self-placed' so that they could escape the abuse.

Sam has now completed an apprenticeship and is proud to be one of 10 selected to compete in the Apprentice of the Year competition. Winning it is very prestigious and comes with great rewards. We're proud to have known Sam and helped them get their qualifications.

INGREDIENTS

Marinade

- 220 g of whole-egg mayonnaise
- 60 g of sour cream or natural yoghurt
- 100 g of tomato paste
- 20 g of lemon juice (about half a small lemon)

METHOD

Chicken

1. Combine the marinade ingredients in a large bowl.
2. Stir in the chicken and onion. Then marinate overnight, covered, in the refrigerator.
3. Spread the marinated chicken in an oven tray. Drizzle with olive oil. Bake at 180°C/350°F/gas mark 4 for about 1 hour, until the chicken is starting to brown on top and is cooked through.
4. Serve the Aleppo chicken on a bed of cooked rice.

- 4 cloves of garlic, crushed
- 10 g of baharat (Middle Eastern seven spice)
- 2 teaspoons of ground paprika (sweet)
- 1 tablespoon of ground cumin
- 1 tablespoon of vegetable stock powder
- ½ teaspoon of salt
- 1 teaspoon of cracked black pepper

To bake

- 1 kg of chicken (breast or thigh), diced
- 2 sliced brown onions
- Drizzle of olive oil

Rice

- 2 cups (400 g) of rice (jasmine works well, but your preferred rice will work too)
- 1 tablespoon of vegetable oil
- 1 teaspoon of vegetable stock powder (or 1 cube)

Rice

1. Rinse the rice until the water is almost clear. Drain.
2. Put the rinsed rice in a heavy-bottomed small saucepan with the tablespoon of vegetable oil and teaspoon of vegetable stock powder. Stir to coat.
3. Cover the rice with enough water to be above the rice by around 2 cm/half an inch/up to your first knuckle.
4. Put the lid on, then bring to the boil. As soon as it's boiling, reduce the heat to a very low simmer for 12 minutes, then turn off. Leave the lid on and let it sit for another 10 minutes. Fluff with a fork.

Garnish (optional)

1. 1 cup (60 g) of slivered almonds, lightly toasted in a pan with a little vegetable oil
2. 1 cup (120 g) of dried cranberries, fried in a pan with a good glug of vegetable oil
3. 1–2 pickled chillies (available from Middle Eastern grocers)

Yoghurt sauce (optional)

- Stir together half a cup (125 ml) of natural yoghurt with half a cup (120 g) of hummus, a good pinch of ground cumin, and a squeeze of lemon juice.

To plate

In a shallow bowl, spread a good helping of cooked rice. Top generously with Aleppo chicken. Finish with a drizzle of yoghurt sauce, then a good tablespoon of each of the toasted almonds and chewy cranberries sprinkled on top. Top with one or two pickled chillies.

Section 3: Building purposeful connections

Over the coming weeks, Howard Buckley invites us to consider the theory, practice wisdom, and his reflections and experiences of making purposeful connections through community building.

Purposeful connections are important in community building. As community builders, we go out of our way to initiate, engage in, and maintain networks of the *kinds of relationships that build community*. We are not social butterflies, striving to keep everyone happy and making the world a prettier place. We are not organizers, getting the 'job done' and done well. We are not charismatic leaders with big followings. We are not the most popular or well-loved community icons who win 'citizen of the year' awards.

We are building community through purposeful connections with others.

Let's not lose sight of this purpose. It is rare enough in our modern world.

Howard is an enthusiastic advocate for the community. He has 30 years of experience in training people to build a better community, in their own ways, in their own part of the world. He knows what works. Howard introduces four key understandings and associated skills that every member of the authors' collective uses every day when building purposeful connections as part of their professional and personal community-building work.

1. **The importance of timing when making connections with others** introduces the skills of 'loitering with intent' and spotting 'opportune moments' when people will be naturally more open to connecting with you.
2. **Go to the people, ask the people, see what the people see** reflects on how our own ways of seeing the world can limit our capacity to see the world from another person's perspective.
3. **Dialogue and holding your agenda lightly** introduces understandings and skills that all the authors use to shape and steer our community-building conversations.
4. **Keywords and common themes** are two key elements that we listen closely for, in order to understand the people we are in dialogue with and where their energy for collective action might come from.

Over these few weeks, we invite you to experiment with integrating these new ideas into your own emerging practice of community building. We offer four experiments in practice for you to adapt to your own community context.

- **Experiment 10. Loitering with intent** will help you hone your skills in watching for opportune moments, so you can make 'natural' connections with people in your wider community who would not otherwise cross your path.
- **Experiment 11. Standing in another person's shoes, seeing what they see** asks you to consciously try to practice seeing someone else's world as they see it, while they are in conversation with you.
- **Experiment 12. Practising your dialogue skills** guides you through two exercises to learn and refine them, applying your skills the next time you have an appropriate conversation.
- **Experiment 13. Identifying common themes** gives you an opportunity to look out for generative themes in a group you are part of, and to observe what happens to the energy of the group when those themes are the focus of conversation.

This section serves as a small masterclass in the core skills of community building. We hope you have found a rhythm in your engagement with this journaling process. We hope previous sections have given you new and useful ways of seeing your wider community. We hope you can begin to integrate these skills into your daily life.

Entry 10: The importance of timing when making connections with others

By Howard Buckley

There is an old joke that a clock was being put in the Leaning Tower of Pisa, because it 'has the inclination but not the time'.

In a similar way, it is one thing to have the intention to connect with others, but another to find the time to make it happen. Yet one of the keys to making effective connections is timing.

Often, people are busy, overwhelmed by their own issues, or even suspicious or afraid. It's challenging to connect with people during these times. However, there are times when people are open and less suspicious, and it is in these moments that we find them receptive to invitations to connect.

Opportune moments for connecting

In the Greek language, there are two words for time: *chronos* and *kairos*. *Chronos* is what we know as clock time – being organized and usually more formal, that is, where we arrange a meeting with someone.

Kairos, however, is the *opportune* time, the 'right' moment, which occurs more informally and organically. In community-building work, identifying *kairos* moments can be particularly helpful in fostering connections.

Dave Andrews, one of the authors in our collective, identifies six types of *kairos* moments when people are more open (Andrews, 1996):

1. Changes, such as when people move house or start a new job.
2. Cycles of life, for example, birth, marriage, death, graduation.
3. Conflict, like disputes between neighbours and groups where people still connect in non-violent and respectful ways despite the conflict.
4. Chance encounters, such as accidents or serendipitous meetings.
5. Celebrations, such as parties, events, and commemorative days.
6. Crises, for example, include emergencies, natural disasters, and illnesses.

Each of these *kairos* moments presents a distinct opportunity for connection. Some are ideal for making new connections with people, especially people who would not otherwise cross your path.

Some are also ideal times for repairing relationships that have been weakened by neglect, damaged by conflict, or where there is suspicion or a lack of trust. You can always wish a grumpy neighbour a 'Merry Christmas', or commiserate cleaning up after a storm, even if your relationship has been frosty for a while.

Everyone is more open to the possibility of a conversation at these opportune moments, provided the invitation to connect is genuine and resonates with the nature of the moment.

Some community workers use the phrase 'loitering with intent' to describe the strategic practice of positioning ourselves in situations where we are more likely to encounter, meet, and capitalize on these kinds of *kairos* moments.

Lisa and the lost puppy

My partner Lisa and I currently live in an apartment, like most people in our neighbourhood. One of the problems with apartment living is that many drive into their garage and disappear into their apartment without entering the street on which they live.

Recently, across the street from our apartment, a girl was visibly upset, looking for her lost puppy. My partner saw this from our balcony and went to help her look for the puppy. Others in the street also became involved.

Through this chance interaction on the street, my partner met a young mum with a baby, living in an apartment across the street, and they began talking. Before long, she had invited the mum and child to our place for a coffee. The *kairos* moment led to exchanging names, phone details, and sharing our stories with each other. Where this connection will lead is unknown.

This story demonstrates the value of being intentional and receptive, having the 'radar on' for those *kairos* moments when circumstances bring an unexpected opportunity.

Lisa was looking for the puppy but also making the most of a *kairos* opportunity to connect. She watched for the kind of person she is interested in getting to know, wandered over, and made a friendly comment about the puppy, which was also an open and receptive invitation to connect.

Making the most of these opportune times for connecting is a foundational skill in community building. With practice, it will come to you as easily and naturally as it did to Lisa. And it will become an indispensable part of your community-building practice toolkit.

P.S. The puppy was found safe and well!

ENTRY 10: THE IMPORTANCE OF TIMING WHEN CONNECTING

REFLECTION

- When you consider the list of six types of *kairos* opportunities, can you picture at least one of each that you have been part of recently?
- What happened each time? What made it a *kairos* moment?
- How could you have made a connection in that moment that you would not otherwise have had the opportunity to?
- Can you identify a way in which you can 'loiter with intent', to help you see the possibility of *kairos* moments?
    - o Common starting points include taking a child to a playground, having a beer at a bar, taking a dog to an off-leash area, running on a popular running route or the area at the start of a bushwalk, joining a crowd listening to a public speaker, or having a smoke at a conference, etc.
    - o There are endless possibilities.

Experiment 10

Loitering with intent

Over the next week, we invite you to make time to practice the twin skills of 'loitering with intent' and 'identifying opportune moments for connecting'.

1. Find a quiet corner at the edge of a public space where there are lots of people coming and going.
2. Identify three 'types' of people who you would like to connect with, who would never cross your path in your day-to-day life.
3. Watch for opportune moments, scanning the people with a soft but attentive gaze and scrolling through Dave's six types of *kairos* moments with an active and engaged imagination.
    - Don't act on them this time, just jot them down, unless your help is really needed in a crisis or a conflict that you can't ignore!

Entry 11: Go to the people, ask the people, see what the people see

By Howard Buckley

For many years, I worked in community settings providing services and programmes for young people. Despite the good intentions of many professionals in these settings, I continually observed them failing to see what young people saw and inadvertently failing to see the young person.

They instead saw what their professional bias, expert learning, programme objectives, and social data had trained them to see. Young people often had to change their stories to fit the service narrative. It was as if they knew the system would not respond to them unless they conformed to its dictates.

We need to see what the people see

One young man, Kyle (not his real name), came to our agency, was very bright and entrepreneurial, yet had been to jail for drug offences and since his release was unemployed and had minimal family support. Most of Kyle's 'case managers' failed to see the world as Kyle saw it; they only saw the 'perceived problems' to be solved. None of the services and programmes offered to Kyle made any real difference.

The failure of service systems to see what the people see is not new. This dilemma was addressed by Rabindranath Tagore (1861–1941), the Bengali winner of the Nobel Prize for Literature in 1913, who invested a significant amount of his time, energy, and family wealth in addressing the poverty he saw in and around Calcutta/Kolkata, India.

Tagore was dismayed at the lack of change his efforts were making, and one day sought to understand why. Importantly, he did not first go to the experts but was inspired to ask the people. The response from the people in the villages was that his efforts had been misguided because he 'did not see what they saw'.

This was profoundly challenging to him yet unlocked a new way of working and has since become a foundational principle for development practice: 'you need to see what the people see'. For a more comprehensive version of this story, see Kelly and Westoby (2018: 62).

In community building, the practice of 'seeing what the people see' enables us to see beyond our own perspectives and build meaningful connections with others. When I met Kyle, I was able to do that, and whole new narratives and possibilities opened, based on his way of seeing the world, and the strengths of resilience and potential he brought into our conversation.

Understanding our own ways of seeing

In a community-building training course that Community Praxis Co-op has run for many years, we often ask participants to brainstorm 'what *prevents* us from seeing what others see' and then, conversely, we ask 'what *helps* us to see what others see'.

The exercise helps us become more aware of when we fail to see and more attentive to practices that enhance our ability to see.

The other side of this coin is the importance of understanding how *we see* the world.

Understanding our own ways of seeing is paramount for building an understanding of the perspectives of others.

In life, we continually *observe* and *interpret* what's happening around us, as Peter explored in entry 3.

When we are looking at anything, we see both a foreground and a background, depending on where we choose to place our focus. When we observe a situation, circumstance, person, or event in our community, we bring the aspects we consider important to the foreground of our attention, allowing those we deem less significant to recede into the background.

For example, the professionals working with Kyle were foregrounding Kyle's problems – from their middle-class, programme-based perspective – and backgrounding his story of resilience and potential. To be effective, they needed to shift their orientation, but to do this, they needed to first recognize how they saw the world.

When our foregrounded perspective causes us to background what is important to others, and we fail to see this, we will struggle to build meaningful connections. We need to exercise care and pay attention to our perspectives, so that we are truly able to see the other person and what they are seeing.

Practice wisdom from the Dalai Lama

The Dalai Lama offers some guidance on this topic in his book, *The Art of Happiness*.

> You may need to be slightly creative. This technique involves the capacity to temporarily suspend insisting on your own viewpoint but rather to look from the other person's perspective, to imagine what would be the situation if you were in his shoes. (Gyatso and Cutler, 1998: 89)

Seeing what others see is an act of imagination and courage, one that reaches beyond the borders of the self and its established views. It is grounded in an attitude of openness and plays out through respectful behaviour towards others.

With the many potential pitfalls and flashpoints you will encounter, *seeing what others see* is an essential starting point when connecting with people with the aim of building community.

REFLECTION

Think of someone with whom you may have a difference. Using your imagination, try seeing the world as if through their eyes.

- Does this reveal that you may not know the person as well as you thought?
- Have you ever enquired about their views, experience, and knowledge?
- Can you envisage a scenario where you could meet with this person and use the opportunity to see what they see? If so, consider how you might approach this creatively.
- Take some time to consider what *helps* and what *hinders* you from seeing things from other people's perspectives.

Experiment 11

Standing in another person's shoes, seeing what they see

Sometime today or tomorrow, when you are in conversation with someone, consciously try to practice *seeing what they see* by experimenting with the technique offered by the Dalai Lama.

1. Imagine you are standing in their shoes, looking at yourself through their eyes, with all their lived experiences informing what they *see in you*.
   - Imagine you are standing in their shoes, looking at the world around you through their eyes, with all their lived experiences informing what they *see in the world*.
   - Imagine you are standing in their shoes, looking at the community you share with them, through their eyes, with all their lived experience informing what they *are seeing in your/their community*.
   - You will become distracted and unconsciously revert to your usual way of viewing the conversation. That's okay.
   - Notice what has happened, and then consciously try to make the shift in your imagination again, to seeing things from their perspective.
2. Reflect on this experience and consider how it might help you build a deeper connection with that person.

Entry 12: Dialogue and holding your agenda lightly

By Howard Buckley

Often, conversations are characterized by a series of monologues, where each person speaks, but there is rarely deep listening and response. This type of communication lacks the depth and reciprocity required to forge deeper connections.

In contrast, a conversational approach that can lead us to a rich and meaningful space of connection is often referred to as dialogue.

Buber's three movements of dialogue

The long-dead German philosopher Martin Buber offers a foundational approach to thinking about dialogue, which we have found very helpful. Buber (1937) says that the practice of dialogue involves three key movements:

1. We present ourselves to the other. For example, this is the simple 'Hello, I am Howard. I've just moved here. Do you live here?.
2. We await and listen to their response. For example, 'Hello Howard, good to meet you. My name is Peter, and I've lived here for a few years'.
3. We respond to their response, which might be something like, 'How have you found living here, Peter?'

These simple yet profound movements to building a purposeful connection with another person.

Creating space for dialogue can be challenging, as we often have blocks and barriers in our communication that hinder it. These could be:

- thinking about what we are going to say next;
- assuming we've heard correctly;
- introducing our own content to shift the direction of the conversation; and
- concluding the conversation, before it has a chance to unfold.

When we practice the three movements of dialogue, we are aiming to create a space of *reciprocal* sharing.

The process of dialogue can unfold at many levels. It always begins with a conversation between individuals, as seen in the example above. It does not gain traction at other levels if we are not using it consistently with individuals.

Community projects built on a solid foundation of ongoing dialogue

As an example of how it can unfold at a community level, I recall a time when I lived in a community where a growing number of refugees were being resettled. My friend and I wanted to make people feel welcome in our neighbourhood, so we approached one of the newly arrived refugees at a local event and introduced ourselves, asking how they were settling in. This was our first movement effort.

Their response and a second movement identified several barriers and potential opportunities related to resettlement in our community.

Our response to their response, a third movement, was to ask if we might meet with other refugees, to hear their stories, and work out ways to support them, which we did, on their turf, over good food, plentiful laughter, and occasional tears.

The dialogue led to the formation of a group of refugees and longer-term locals, which was soon engaged in setting up homes with furniture and household items as new families arrived in our neighbourhood, making their resettlement journey easier. The group could move into action mode quickly and easily because it was built on a solid foundation of ongoing dialogue.

Holding your agenda lightly

When practising dialogue, we have also learned how important it is to hold our agenda lightly.

As an example of this, consider the following story. Sue had moved into a small apartment complex and was eager to meet with other residents in her area. She invited everyone over for a morning tea.

To do this, initially, she left a written invitation on doorsteps, but to her disappointment, nobody attended. Sue was also a keen gardener and often placed seedlings she had collected on her veranda to catch the sunshine.

One day, a neighbour noticed her watering the seedlings. He asked her about the seedlings, as he also grew them, which led to them sharing seedlings and gardening ideas. Some of the other neighbours got involved in the discussion too.

Ironically, for Sue, once she stopped trying to bring people together via the written invitation and instead held her agenda 'lightly', people found a way of coming together around her. When Sue held her agenda lightly, she connected with neighbours through an opportunistic moment (see the previous reflection on *kairos* moments) that enabled her to more naturally invite her neighbours in for a cup of tea.

Dialogue cannot be rushed, and practising the 'three movements' while 'holding your agenda lightly' will certainly improve the likelihood of creating both depth and effectiveness in your connections (Westoby and Dowling, 2009).

REFLECTION

- How could you use dialogue to open spaces of reciprocal sharing in your community-building conversations?
- What do you learn from Sue's story that will inform your future community-building efforts?

Experiment 12

Practising your dialogue skills

This week, we ask you to practise the three movements of dialogue discussed above. It can be challenging, so we've provided detailed instructions to guide you through the process. Please persevere – these are core skills for successful community builders.

Remember, this will be clunky, like the first time you rode a bike or drove a car. But the clunkiness means you are learning. You are beyond your usual way of holding a conversation and are on a learning curve. If it isn't clunky, you are not learning!

Practise staying with their content

1. Next time you get a good opportunity for a conversation, practise 'staying with another person's content' by applying the following 'rules of engagement':
   - Remain focused entirely on what the other person says and only respond to their content.
   - Don't introduce any of your content.
   - Don't interpret or change the course of the conversation.
2. At the end of the conversation, reflect on the following:
   - What did you have to consciously remind yourself of 'what to do' and 'not to do'?
   - Consider any feedback the other person might have given you during or at the end of the exchange.
   - Identify implications for how you might want to modify your approach for future conversations with others.

Practise the three movements of dialogue

When you have mastered the art of staying with the other person's agenda, you will be able to practise Buber's three movements of dialogue.

1. Next time you get a good opportunity for a conversation, practise the three movements of dialogue with someone in your neighbourhood, group, or workplace.
    - First, initiate a conversation with a simple statement about yourself that indicates something you might have in common with them, then add a simple, similar question about them, related to what you have just revealed about yourself. (Look carefully at the example above. This is the first movement.)
    - Then listen to their response (This is the second movement, but it comes from them, and it is entirely out of your control. It is what it is.)
    - Third, carefully respond to their response, no matter what it is. What you want is to demonstrate understanding. (This is the third movement.)
2. For the rest of the conversation, repeat the same kinds of processes, as appropriate, staying with what they are expressing, and holding your own agenda lightly.
    - If their responses from then on are all entirely self-involved, there will be limited opportunity for mutual dialogue.
    - But, if at some point they ask you a question about one of your responses, you have made a breakthrough and dialogue is possible.
    - Then, you respond carefully, give a genuine response to their question, then end by asking them a question, often how they feel about, or what they think about, what you've just said.
    - If nothing else comes to mind, you can just make it something like 'But I'm not really sure, what do you think?'

3. When you get home, reflect on these experiences. Consider whether the practice opens up any possibilities, clears any blockages, or brings clarity to any problems in your connection with that person or group.

Entry 13: Keywords and common themes

By Howard Buckley

Having explored the transformative power of dialogue and 'holding our agendas lightly' in the last reflection, we now turn our attention to two key ideas within the art of listening: listening for 'keywords' and listening for 'common themes'.

Listening for keywords

Keywords are a significant part of what we listen for when in dialogue. Keywords are what join us as humans when communicating, yet often we misunderstand one another because we fail to inquire what someone means by their keyword.

For example, if we ask someone how they are doing, and they reply with the simple keyword 'okay', we generally know what they mean. That's the 'joining' role of keywords.

Yet, at the same time, we do not specifically know what 'okay' means to that person. Hence, we often need to enter dialogue around their keywords.

This is true in most dialogues. People use keywords that invite us to join them in a shared experience or value or common cause – words like 'love', 'justice', 'hope', 'isolation', 'tired', or 'angry' are just a few examples. Yet we do not know what they actually mean unless we ask.

By paying close attention to when people use keywords and collectively exploring their shared meaning, opportunities are created for genuine discussions and the unlocking of energies for change. For example, if someone says, 'I am angry with the government' or 'I am angry with that community group', we generally understand what 'angry' means. However, we need to engage in more dialogue and listen to truly understand. We could ask, 'What is it that you are angry about?'

Keywords can also have an 'energizing' role in community building. When people discuss what is important to them, we need to focus on their keywords, and we can shape a dialogue that builds narratives around those concepts.

Often, keywords have a problem element embedded in them, but sometimes the keywords will appear as aspiration statements laden with hopes and dreams, or they can be expressions about what excites and inspires people.

That's where more possibilities open to connect with people, and we cultivate purposeful relationships from there.

Listening for common themes

The second idea in this reflection is that we are also listening for 'common themes'.

Common themes represent concerns, issues, or dreams that are shared within a community. They are themes that are recurring, as we listen to different people. It's a sure sign that we're onto something, where there's shared energy to have collective conversations and consider mutual actions.

For example, in the 1980s, the government planned to build a radioactive waste dump in an outer suburb of Brisbane. Community consultation by the government was limited, but as the news spread across the affected neighbourhoods, discussions emerged with questions such as 'where will it be built?', 'why in our area?', 'how safe will it be?', or 'what are the risks for our children?'

There were far more questions than answers, and many people in the neighbourhood were not happy about the proposal. It was a *kairos* moment for our whole suburb. A public meeting was arranged by the local neighbourhood centre, where I was involved, to hear from residents. An array of concerns and fears were expressed, and key phrases like 'radioactive waste dump' and 'our government is not listening to us' were repeated by different people. These common themes became catalysts for people to come together, to act publicly, not only to stop the dump but also to give voice to their community's aspirations.

This story is an example of how keywords and the common themes that emerge from a situation can be harnessed as catalysts that energize people to take collective action about the situation.

Listening for keywords and common themes is a crucial tool for fostering meaningful connections with others and driving action in our communities.

REFLECTION

Identify a group of people whom you meet regularly.

Take a moment to think about the last time you were talking with them and some of the matters they raised that were important to them.

Perhaps the conversation got a little heated. However, there was definitely a spark of energy among at least a few members of the group.

- Can you recall the keywords they used? Jot them down if so.
- Can you remember how others responded to those keywords?
- Can you imagine how you could have responded differently to those keywords?
- How might those keywords influence how you proceed in your relationship with that group?

Experiment 13

Identifying common themes

Think about the conversation that you just reflected on.

1. Jot down all phrases that were repeated, that appeared to energize or enliven the conversation:
   - as best you remember them (put aside any interpretation or judgement);
   - just jot them down, as the people expressed them.
2. Take a short walk, then return to the page. Read them out loud, listening closely for any depth of meaning they might convey.
   - Consider these phrases as a whole. Are they collectively saying something?
   - Then jot down what you consider to be the three key common themes to come out of the group's conversation.
3. Next time you meet with that group, look for opportunities to use those phrases in your contribution to the conversation, one at a time, at appropriate moments. Or watch for when others use them, in case they beat you to it.
4. Observe the group's energy levels as the phrase is introduced into the conversation.
   - If it goes up, you can be confident you've identified a common theme for that group.
   - If they are flat, you've missed the mark on that one

Recipe
Dips

Prep time: 5–10 minutes.
Serves 4-6.

Easy-peasy 'hummus'

Vegan; gluten free if necessary.

This is the kind of dip you can whip up in a flash, using ingredients typically found in your pantry. Perfect for those last-minute 'bring a plate' morning teas. I put hummus in quotation marks because it's so far removed from traditional hummus recipes. Depending on the juiciness of your lemon and the type of soy sauce you use, you may need to adjust these quantities to suit your taste. Remember, you can always add more, but once it's in, it's hard to get out. Serve with carrot sticks and rice crackers or crisp pita.

INGREDIENTS

- 2 cans of chickpeas, drained and rinsed
- 3 tablespoons of olive oil
- 3 tablespoons of lemon juice
- 2 tablespoons of dark soy sauce (check if yours is gluten free)

METHOD

1. Put all the ingredients in a food processor and whizz until smooth (about 5 minutes). Stop to scrape the sides of the bowl occasionally. Taste for flavour along the way.

Tzatziki

INGREDIENTS

- 2 cups (500 g) natural Greek yoghurt
- Half a Lebanese cucumber, coarsely grated
- 2 tablespoons of fresh lemon juice
- 4 cloves of garlic, crushed
- 1 teaspoon of salt
- 4 tablespoons of fresh mint, finely diced

METHOD

1. Start by grating the cucumber into a bowl, then sprinkle it with salt and let it sit while you gather the remaining ingredients. Toss occasionally.
2. Squeeze the excess water out of the cucumber using a sieve, a clean tea towel, or a paper towel.
3. Add all the ingredients together in a bowl and stir until well combined.

Cheese and tomato dip

Vegetarian; gluten free.

My mum has made this dip ever since I can remember, so it's not a new recipe to me. I have never seen anyone else make it, though. It sometimes appears on our catering dips platter, and when it does, it gets great reviews. Fair warning, though, it's very moreish.

INGREDIENTS

- 250 g of cream cheese
- ⅓ cup (90 g) of tomato sauce
- 1 small onion, finely diced
- 2 tablespoons of red capsicum/pepper, finely diced
- 2 tablespoons of chopped parsley
- Salt and pepper, to taste

METHOD

1. Put all the ingredients into the bowl of a kitchen mixer and beat until well combined.

Section 4: Building small groups

Section 3 focused on building purposeful relationships. In community building, we usually build such relationships so that we can bring people together into small groups. This is the creative and powerful movement from I to we (two people) to us (a group).

In a healthy, thriving community, we hear people talking about 'our' and 'us' all the time. When we start something new, we know we're making progress when others in the group begin using these terms to describe their experience and involvement in it, whatever it might be.

We conduct most of our community-building work within and with groups, engaging others in collaborative conversations and modelling healthy ways of being and processes for community life. In those groups, we are often the ones who are most attentive to a healthy group process and to group life over time. More and more you will be, too, as you gain confidence and experience.

In this section, Richard Warner invites us into his experience of working with small groups – a key part of the development, consolidation, and ongoing life of the Nundah Community Enterprises Co-operative, in Brisbane, Australia.

For Richard, small, inclusive groups where people understand the shared nature of their experiences thrive through a simple methodology that supports ongoing mutual action, transforming the communities they are part of. He invites us to reflect on:

1. **Small groups: the heartbeat of community** describes the way healthy communities all have one thing in common: the presence of vibrant and diverse small groups of engaged people.
2. **Small is beautiful, and inclusion is the key** reminds us of the importance of retaining a human scale and holistic vision, where the uniqueness of local people, social contexts, and environments are valued.
3. **Movement from a private to a shared concern** describes a crucial shift in community building, from 'I am isolated and feeling lonely' to 'many of us are isolated and there is a pandemic of loneliness'. This shift from 'I' to 'we' is one of the foundations of our community-building practice.
4. **Building small groups through the 0–1–3 method** introduces us to the 0–1–3 methodology, one of the most important concepts in this journal. This simple yet subtle methodology is a cornerstone of the

community-building work that all of us in the author's collective have undertaken, in various contexts around the world, over more than 30 years.

In the practice experiments in this section, Richard invites us to reflect on the small groups we are already involved in, and the ways we currently contribute to them, and to experiment with new ways of engaging.

- **Experiment 14. Heightening the consciousness of a group; or step towards one** asks you to either consider a group you are a part of with some fresh new eyes, or take a step towards joining one.
- **Experiment 15. Opening up one group** asks you to consider how you might help one small group you are part of to open up to the wider community and become more inclusive of diverse people.
- **Experiment 16. Moving from private concern to shared action** invites you to identify a challenge in your life that is out of your control and where you feel you are to blame, then to reframe the challenge from how you experience it as an isolated individual to how you might understand it when others have also experienced it.
- **Experiment 17. Finding two others to work with** guides you through the beginnings of a community-building process, centred around a concern you have about an issue in your wider community. It starts the way the authors always do – by finding two others to work with, who share your concerns, values, and approach to community.

This section should equip you with effective and strategic community-building skills that the author's collective uses all the time in our personal and professional community work practice.

You can learn more about Nundah Community Enterprises Co-operative at www.ncec.com.au.

Entry 14: Small groups: the heartbeat of community

By Richard Warner

Healthy communities, from the humblest to the most impressive, all have one thing in common: the presence of vibrant and diverse small groups of engaged people. The often-quoted unverified words of Margaret Mead, as mentioned in the introduction, are worth remembering:

> Never doubt that a small group of thoughtful committed individuals can change the world. In fact, it's the only thing that ever has.

Our small groups are a microcosm of community

Why is the small group so important? Because it's a microcosm of the community, a safe space where individuals can enter, be listened to, and learn to listen to others. It's a place where our individual stories are respectfully held, but also where they can miraculously converge in the 'aha' of a shared understanding. Importantly, it's a place where we take the first tentative steps of meaningful action together. We find courage to be ourselves with others in a small group, in a way that just isn't possible in bigger groups.

While this can be true, it might make the process of participating in small groups sound idyllic, which it often isn't! A wonderful description compares the process to the polishing of rocks in a tumbler. When working closely with others, we inevitably encounter friction, particularly when we come up against our rough edges. The process of relating in the safe container of a group helps us polish those edges, live with our differences, and even come to value these edges and their unique characteristics. The inner qualities of the stone, so to speak, are revealed. It's worth mentioning that, in healthy small groups, difficulties and differences are never plastered over, but we do get more comfortable negotiating them and may even come to see them as generative. The opportunity to learn in this way is one of the privileges of working in small groups.

The Nundah Workers' Co-operative Speakers' Group

In the Nundah Workers' Co-operative, one of our small groups calls itself the Speakers' Group. Our workers come together there to share stories of their past experiences seeking employment as people with a disability, and to reflect on why they started or joined the cooperative in the first place. They also plan to present their story at conferences and share it through social media.

Powerful stories – both heartbreaking and heartwarming – are shared within this group, which have inspired others to start their own social enterprises and challenge and inspire us to stay the course. The Speakers' Group plays a crucial role in reminding us of the importance of continuing to create inclusive workplaces.

After 15 years of managing a social enterprise, where people with and without disability create an inclusive work community, I've learned that small groups are not just the starting point of a community process; they must be nourished along the way – woven and rewoven into the fabric of community, because they are a central thread.

REFLECTION

- What small groups are you already a part of in your community?
    - o   Consider those that have a name, as well as those that don't.
- What has been your experience, both positive and negative, in these groups?
- What do you think contributes to the functioning of a healthy, small group?
    - o   Are there any key wisdoms or principles you think are important to the functioning of a small group?
- Small groups will often form around shared agendas. What need might there be for a new small group in your community?

Experiment 14

Heightening the consciousness of a group; or step towards one

This week is an opportunity to bring a new consciousness to a group you might be a part of, or to take a step towards joining a group you have had in mind.

1. If you are already a part of a group, think about how you can bring your reflections into a broader conversation with others in the group.
2. At a timely moment, let the group know you have been using this journal to reflect on wisdoms and principles that make for a well-functioning group. Ask them to each do the same as the steps above and identify some collective wisdoms.
3. Share and discuss these wisdoms as a group, and take some time to consider how to improve the culture or functioning of this group; that is, activate some of those agreed wisdoms.
4. If you are not part of a group, perhaps this is the week to take a tentative step towards joining one. Is there a group you have imagined joining?
5. Ask someone who is an active member (or reach out through the contact page if there is one) whether you could come and be an observer. See if the group is one that behaves according to at least some or most of the wisdoms or principles that you have identified as a healthy group.
6. After that observation, consider whether this is a group where you could invest some of your time and energy, or if you need to explore another one.

Entry 15: Small is beautiful, and inclusion is the key

By Richard Warner

A little over 50 years ago, the famous book by Ernst Schumacher, *Small is Beautiful: Economics as if People Mattered* (1973), was published. Even if you haven't read it, you are likely to have heard its title, such is the impact of the work. Movements such as farmers' markets, buy-local programmes, and community enterprises have been inspired by its vision of an alternative to large-scale processes that lose touch with the localities they were meant to serve.

In building community, 'small is beautiful' reminds us of the importance of retaining a human scale and a holistic vision, where the uniqueness of local people, social contexts, and environments are valued.

Nundah Workers' Co-operative: small enough to listen deeply to one another

In the case of our Nundah Workers' Co-operative, 'small is beautiful' meant the beautiful work of listening deeply to members with disabilities. At the time of our founding in 1998, a significant amount of government funding was available for transitional programmes to help people transition into the workforce. However, our members' experience was that these programmes were a dead end. Despite good intentions, jobs in the competitive labour market were not designed to include workers with a disability, and they repeatedly, in their words, 'got the sack'.

What our members really wanted was a workplace where there was respect for their gifts and accommodation of their needs – a long-term solution. This meant we had to start small and work with local relationships and resources, and sometimes refuse the funds offered by state-funded programmes.

Our model of organic growth, based on listening to people, has evolved into a large organization and sustained livelihoods for over 25 years. Small indeed has proved beautiful.

Staying small and inclusive

When we think small, we mean the size of, say, three to 12 people. A group could literally start with three people getting together and doing the beautiful work of listening to one another. Then it might grow. Some of the best groups I have been a part of consist of five to seven people. That's small enough that everyone can sit around the table and relate to each other mutually, relationally, and respectfully. People don't need to compete to be heard, and silence is noticed with a gentle, 'How are you doing? Inclusion is the key to effective small group work.

There's nothing inherently wrong, of course, with having larger groups to solve a problem or taking on funding appropriate to a community cause. However, when we overlook local realities, we risk repeating the very issues we set out to address.

Enabling the inclusion of all voices, especially those often overlooked, ensures that, regardless of the scale of our activity, we remain attuned to what is truly happening on the ground. This is why 'small is beautiful' will remain a touchstone for generations to come.

ENTRY 15: SMALL IS BEAUTIFUL, AND INCLUSION IS THE KEY

REFLECTION

- Close your eyes for a second and remember what it feels like when you have been listened to and included.
- Consider practical steps you can take in relationships or within your community to foster a culture of inclusion.

Experiment 15

Opening up one group

Small groups can sometimes be too inward-looking and become 'stuck'. This experiment asks you to consider how you might help one small group you are part of to open up to the wider community and become more inclusive of diverse people.

1. Choose one small group that you are part of.
   - Reflect on the types of people involved and who else might benefit from participating.
   - Consider some gentle ways to steer the group's current conversations, building awareness of the diversity present in your wider community.
2. Try these strategies next time you meet.
   - Note any resistance, or even hostility, and just let it slide.
   - Look for those other members who are most receptive to your approach.
3. Initiate individual conversations with supportive group members about friends they have who might benefit from being part of the group.
4. When they identify someone, ask what it would take for them to feel comfortable inviting that person along? And, if you can, assure them that you will do your best to overcome any barriers, and that you will join them in making sure their friend feels welcome.
5. If no one can identify anyone, you are probably wasting your time with that group. You are probably better off focusing your attention on another group.

Entry 16: Movement from a private to a shared concern

By Richard Warner

There are movements that occur within the building of community, which are markers of a healthy process – signs that it has dynamism and life.

One of these is the movement from 'I' to 'we', a humble but seismic shift, where we break free from an isolated viewpoint and acknowledge we are 'in it together'.

Related to this is the shift from a 'private concern' to a 'shared concern'. It is not an overstatement to say that this change of perspective is the lifeblood of a community process and critical to all collective change efforts. For example, it is the shift from 'I am isolated and feeling lonely' to 'many of us are isolated and there is a pandemic of loneliness'.

Nundah Workers' Co-operative: a shift from I to we

At Nundah Workers' Co-operative, it is the shift from 'I am unemployed and must be stupid' to 'we are unemployed because people with disabilities are too often excluded'. Notice the shift from 'I' to 'we'. Why is this perspective shift important? Moving from a private (I) to a shared (we) concern connects us with others and broadens our view. It helps us move beyond a first-person perspective to see the broader landscape of our situation. It can be transformative in our understanding of the problems we face and remind us of what we collectively hold dear.

If you tap its energy, it will power the process of community building in a way that is far more valuable than any grant or donation.

The story of Food Connect Shed

The power of shifting from a private to a shared concern is clear in the story of Food Connect Shed, an organization that has been a catalyst in Australia's fair food movement, providing small-scale producers with access to fair prices. Founder Rob Pekin has a powerful story of moving from a place of isolation and despair to one that is connected and impassioned.

Rob is a fourth-generation dairy farmer who lost his farm upon the deregulation of the dairy industry a quarter of a century ago. This was devastating to his sense of identity and purpose. It was not until he went on a road trip and began to speak with other farmers in a similar plight that he realized he was not alone and not to blame. Out of this shared understanding (the I to we) arose the belief that 'a local economy that works for all is possible'.

Inspired by this reframing of the problem he had experienced, Rob began the process of connecting with small-scale farmers and city dwellers who wanted to support them. Together, they formed Food Connect, a food hub and distribution centre that brought together local regional suppliers with their 'city cousins' or purchasers (Food Connect Shed, 2025).

Food Connect is at the forefront of community-supported agriculture in Australia, continually innovating to provide alternatives to large-scale, environmentally harmful farming practices. A story born of individual despair has turned to one of collective flourishing, all through the flash of recognition that *my* private problem is also *our* shared problem, and that what is could also be otherwise.

ENTRY 16: MOVEMENT FROM A PRIVATE TO A SHARED CONCERN

REFLECTION

- How does the movement from 'I to we' change things?
- What can you learn from this story about the Nundah Workers' Co-operative?
- What can you learn from the story of Food Connect?

Experiment 16

Moving from private concern to shared action

1. Identify a challenge in your life that is beyond your control and where you feel you are to blame.
2. Consider what it would feel like if others told you they had a very similar experience.
3. Reframe the challenge from how you experience it as an isolated individual to how you might understand it when numerous others have also faced the same experience.
4. As the shared challenge is acknowledged, does it seem possible to you that a shared agenda for change might arise from it? How would this happen?
5. Identify some possible initial steps towards shared action.

Entry 17: Building small groups through the 0–1–3 method

By Richard Warner

A constant theme in this reflective journal is that 'going it alone' makes community building very hard. In a sense, going it alone means having no relationships. It's the space of I, me, my idea, what I'd like to do.

The obvious next step after being alone is to find another person and have a conversation. This opens up the possibility that I can shift to we, and 'my idea' can become 'our idea'.

Sometimes, this two-person relationship is described as a dyad. It's the 0–1 part of a 0–1–3 triad. Two people, but, importantly, linked by only one relationship. In our experience, two people linked by one relationship is rarely a strong enough 'structure' for stability and sustainability.

We therefore prefer the minimal structure of a triad, symbolized as 0–1–3.

> A threefold cord is not easily broken. (*Ecclesiastes* 4:12)

The 0–1–3 method of building community

The 0–1–3 method is a shorthand way of describing this basic building block of small groups in community (Kelly and Westoby, 2018). At risk of repeating, the numbers indicate human relationships: where there is one person, there are no relationships (0), where there are two people, there is one relationship (1), and where there are three people, there are three relationships (3). In community building, it is the *quality* of the relationships that is crucial. This is the basic building block of community. Three people, linked by three strong, open, mutual relationships.

The 0–1–3 method provides a framework for thinking about the basic steps in building community. We begin with ourselves in isolation (no relationships), then listen to and connect with another in dialogue (two people, hence one relationship). A quantum leap occurs when we come together as three – that triad – and identify as a set of relationships with a common identity. Think of 0–1–3 as the minimum set of conditions required for a community process to begin. You could think of it as the 'power of three'.

It takes three points to form the first and strongest geometric form, and in human terms, when three work together, there is a strength that arises beyond that of a single dyadic relationship.

With three relationships, for the first time, there are another two relationships able to assist if a relationship breaks down – and, importantly, no one can easily control the whole, as there is at least one relationship independent of them.

This is crucial. Please pause and think about it.

How the 0–1–3 methodology was used to start the Nundah Workers' Co-operative

A 0–1–3 method was critical to the development of Nundah Co-operative. It began humbly when a community worker listened deeply to a number of young people with disabilities. He noticed that their stories centred around the feeling of rejection of not having a job.

He took the uncommon step of not providing a solution but rather inviting them to meet to share their stories. Through this invitation, the young people developed their own solution to address a common concern.

A 0–1–3 group was formed, which was then expanded with a few more people. Together, they formed a small 'jobs club', which has since grown into a thriving community business, governed by its members and still employing them 25 years later, along with many others.

As expressed in this story, a single 0–1–3 often becomes incredibly powerful when it connects its participants to an ever-widening web of relationships, which, like a spider's web, strengthens as each new relationship – a strand between an existing and a new node of connection – is added.

The 0–1–3 method reduces the risk of self-centredness and requires trust and sharing in the building of a common identity. It breaks open our isolation and can address our powerlessness. A 0–1–3 is a microcosm and marker of community.

Beyond three

The strength of groups built using the 0–1–3 approach comes from the number of relationships that independently hold the group together. A group of four people can have up to six strong relationships holding it together; a group of five can have 10; six can have 15; and the number of potential relationships grows exponentially.

We can strengthen triads by unearthing shared agendas and linking group members who share a common interest, concern, or skill. The strongest groups we are part of share multiple agendas, including social, economic, and cultural.

Furthermore, the real strength lies in the number of active triads that work simultaneously, both autonomously and collaboratively, to achieve the group's goals. It is a structure with huge potential.

REFLECTION

- Think of some examples of 0–1–3 triads in your life (family, friends, workplace, or community). Journal these if you like, or unpack them through the following questions.
    o What brought these groups together, and what keeps them together?
    o If one of these 0–1–3 triads broke down, what might have helped to repair and sustain it?
    o There can also be a natural ending to 0–1–3 triads, as they disband, and participants move on to other places, people, and causes. What is a healthy way to celebrate and mark the end of a 0–1–3 connection?

Experiment 17

Finding two others to work with

This week, you get to practise the skill of connecting with others about a shared concern.

1. What are some of the small, but nonetheless important, concerns that have been forgotten in your community? Continue writing until you are satisfied.
2. Take a moment to review your list. Identify three that resonate most strongly for you that you might like to be involved in addressing.
3. Identify which one of these three you think might resonate with others; in other words, which might be a shared concern?
4. Identify at least two other people who might like to join you in attending to this concern in the way described above.

Recipe
Spiced cauliflower salad bowl

Prep time: 30–40 minutes. **Cooking time:** 1 hour.
Serves 4.

Moya is a valuable member of the Nundah Co-operative and arguably one of the healthiest! She walks everywhere and researches everything she puts in and on her body. She's been with Nundah Co-operative since the early days and recalls, 'We all wanted to work, so we started making sandwiches'. Before she started working at the Nundah Co-operative, she said 'people would help her *get* a job, but wouldn't help her *in* the job'. Moya feels that there should be a greater variety of jobs for people with learning difficulties.

INGREDIENTS

Spiced roasted cauliflower

- 1 head of cauliflower
- 2 tablespoons of harissa sauce (or less if you're not keen on spice)
- 1 ½ tablespoons of cumin
- 2 tablespoons of turmeric
- 2 tablespoons of paprika
- 1 tablespoon of vegetable stock powder
- ½ cup (125 ml) of vegetable oil

For the salad bowl

- 2 baby cos lettuce, shredded
- 1 punnet of cherry tomatoes, halved
- Half a Lebanese cucumber, cut into cubes or slices
- Thinly sliced red onion, pickled in enough white vinegar to just cover the onion, with a pinch of salt and a teaspoon of sugar
- 1 cup (240 g) of hummus (store bought or see the recipe in section 3)
- 1 cup (240 g) of tzatziki (store bought or see the recipe in section 3)
- 2 pita bread or flatbread: cut into eight triangles, spray with oil, season with salt and pepper, bake in the oven for 7–10 minutes until crispy
- Lemon, cut in half, then sliced. For an added touch, lightly heat the lemon in a pan on both sides to bring out some sweetness

METHOD

1. Preheat the oven to 170°C/350°F/gas mark 4
2. Cut the cauliflower into small florets and put in a large baking tray.
3. Sprinkle the cauliflower with the remaining ingredients and toss to coat.
4. Bake in the oven for 1 hour until tender and starting to brown.
5. While you are waiting, prepare the salad items.
6. To assemble the bowls:
    - add a large handful of lettuce;
    - stand the toasted pita on one side of the bowl;
    - top the lettuce with sections of cherry tomatoes, cucumber, and cauliflower;
    - spoon on a good amount of hummus and tzatziki;
    - top with pickled onion and grilled lemon slices.

Section 5: Sustaining groups

Over the next few weeks of our journey, Richard Warner and Howard Buckley introduce us to practices and wisdom on how to make the groups we are involved in more sustainable.

They invite us to reflect on four topics:

1. **What sustains groups?** This looks at, in particular, the importance of a shared agenda or purpose, shared collaborative processes, and a shared commitment to action for healthy, participatory community groups.
2. **Stages of group development**, using the five stages model: forming, storming, norming, performing, and mourning. It's old, but it's good.
3. **Sustaining groups when things get stuck or conflict arises** are skills that all community builders will need. Richard walks us through simple but profoundly effective practice wisdom that makes a real difference.
4. **Allowing groups to die well** is crucial for making room for renewal in community life. We all need to improve at letting go, and rituals and celebrations can be particularly helpful.

These reflections are important because much of our work in building community is done in groups with others.

They include experiments that will equip you to take on a leadership role when the groups you are involved in need your help.

- **Experiment 18. A group health and sustainability 'check-in'** suggests that you facilitate a reflection on the sustainability of a group you are involved in and have a long-term commitment to.
- **Experiment 19. Facilitating a group to map a shared timeline of their experience** by mapping the group's life together and discussing how the five stages of group development help make sense of it.
- **Experiment 20. Imagining yourself as an excellent group conflict resolver** asks you to put aside your current self-image and imagine what you would do to address conflict in a group if you had a great understanding and skills.
- **Experiment 21. Celebrating the end of a group** invites you to design a celebration, including an appropriate ritual, for the ending of a group you have been part of.

We hope this section leaves you feeling more informed about the process of group life and the interventions that might be helpful to the group at key moments in its life cycle.

Entry 18: What sustains groups?

By Howard Buckley

In earlier sections, we discussed how small groups create the foundation for community change. Often, a single idea or concern sparks the formation of these groups, but a key factor in their sustainability is the ability to share responsibilities.

Unlike groups with a central leader or coordinator, the kinds of groups we love are characterized by a shared agenda, collaborative processes, and a collective commitment to action. I refer to this as the **ABC** of a participatory group:

1. a shared **A**genda to do something together;
2. creating a shared **B**asis of how people work together; and
3. a shared **C**ommitment to action.

In this reflection, we will explore how we can sustain our groups using these three practices.

Finding a way around the bureaucracy, together

I knew a group of parents who were concerned about their children's safety while walking to the school bus stop along a rural road with no footpaths. This made the trip each school day potentially dangerous for their children. Steadily, the neighbourhood group grew, with the aim of improving safety for their children.

At first, they asked the local council to build a footpath, and when that failed, they didn't give up; instead, they continued to work together to explore other ways to achieve it. Their shared purpose was strong.

Holding a weekly gathering for social drinks became an informal and enjoyable way for the group to stay in touch and invite others in the neighbourhood to join them. The social drinks became invaluable for the group to build trust and purpose in their relationships, to discuss their strategies and plan actions. It established the foundation for their discussion. As others joined and discussion flowed, it enabled a steady flow of information and became a catalyst for ideas and action.

At one of the social gatherings, a parent noticed children jumping over the fences to get to each other's houses. It sparked an idea that maybe they didn't need a public footpath after all: they could create a path through their yards to access the bus stop.

Excitement and energy increased, and others became involved; projects began to replace sections of fences with gates. The shared commitment to action ensured the group's sustainability for even longer.

The things that help sustain any small group

Every time I ask the question 'what sustains your group?' in community training courses, the characteristics raised can be located under these three headings:

- shared purpose;
- shared collaborative processes; and
- a shared commitment to action.

If these elements become core practices in a group, the sustainability of the group will not be dependent on strong personalities, individual leadership, or access to external resources. It will be sustained by shared participation, with a focus on building trusting and supportive relationships within the group.

When asked what helps build this in groups, the answers are usually voiced as very simple and human responses:

- sharing meals together;
- making space for fun, creativity, and laughter;
- individually checking in with how people are feeling;
- showing care and support to group members as required;
- being attentive to changes occurring for group members; and
- celebrating group achievements.

Often, I am one of the people paying most attention to the group processes and the health and vibrancy of a group. Another key in my own practice is noticing what already energizes and enlivens a group and nurturing those things.

As you become more engaged in intentional community building, you may find that you are one of the people who takes more notice of what the group needs and show more care for those who are on the margins of the group, in various ways.

ENTRY 18: WHAT SUSTAINS GROUPS?

REFLECTION

- Think of groups you've been part of that were positive experiences. List what was happening under the headings of:
    o shared agenda or purpose;
    o shared collaborative processes;
    o shared commitment to action;
    o anything else you think is really important.
- Reflect on the extent to which your experiences match with Howard's ABC idea.
- How could these things be nurtured in groups you are currently involved in?

Experiment 18

A group health and sustainability 'check-in'

This experiment asks you to take some responsibility for the ongoing health and sustainability of a group you are committed to, in the long term.

1. Next time the group meets, tell them about the journal (if you haven't already) and the three keys for group health and sustainability.
2. Ask if they'd like to reflect on the life of their group, using this framework, and facilitate that discussion.
3. If possible, turn these group reflections into a plan for sustaining your group. It doesn't have to be a large or complex plan but, rather, something your group can use to conduct a regular 'sustainability health' check-up.

Entry 19: Stages of group development

By Howard Buckley

When we considered what sustains groups, we focused on the 'how to' of group development. In this reflection, we will explore the stages that groups experience to increase our awareness of what can happen over the life cycle of a community group.

In 1965, Bruce Tuckman identified four key stages of group development: forming, storming, norming, and performing. In 1977, he added a fifth: adjourning or mourning.

As with all good frameworks, these stages are not meant to be prescriptive; rather, they serve as a helpful descriptor. They are also not always linear but, often, circular. Many have elaborated on this basic framework to assist their work with groups.

Forming

When groups are forming, they are usually characterized by politeness and care as group members get to know each other. M. Scott Peck (1987) called this 'pseudo-community', and while there is an element of inauthenticity, it is necessary so members feel welcome and comfortable being part of the group. It enables a group to build a foundation for exploring relationships, values, and purpose, and to establish fundamental processes in a safe and supportive manner.

Storming

As differences emerge between participants, it usually doesn't take long for groups to enter the storming stage, as members push their own agendas or personalities clash and conflict looms.

Sometimes groups don't survive this stage, as it becomes too difficult (or chaotic) and members leave, or they revert to 'pseudo-community', as it seems easier. This cycle between forming and storming often leads to more harmful results, as loud voices dominate, or the whole group's agendas are narrowed too quickly.

The storming, however painful, is necessary for the group to move out of fight-or-flight modes and discover a third option – acceptance and negotiation. Then the group can develop.

Norming

The norming stage follows, during which the group learns ways to resolve differences, hear diverse voices, and hold their agendas lightly enough to build a shared agenda. Roles and tasks are clarified, and shared decision-making emerges. This calls for members to empty themselves of pushing agendas and being in control and make space for others.

Don't be afraid of the emptiness that often follows group conflict. It is the space that will enable the group to create 'norms' that build resilience and more lasting cooperative action.

Performing

Once norming is in place, a group can then perform. The group, at this stage, has successfully combined a focus on both tasks and relationships, resulting in the achievement of its purpose. Plans are set, goals are met, and people enjoy being part of the group.

A performing group will demonstrate reciprocity and care between its members and is often accompanied by a desire from others to join the group.

An often-forgotten action amongst community groups in this stage is the celebration of their achievements, both small and large.

Mourning

The final stage of group development occurs when members either leave the group or it decides to disband, and mourning is required. Endings require attention, as does honouring the grief and loss of a group member who has contributed.

If the group has come to an end, members need processes to accept this, including celebrating what they have achieved together.

Embracing the changing 'seasons of the group' will require 'little mourning's' in order for renewal and regeneration to take place.

The authors frequently utilize this framework to help groups understand their journey. Whatever stage of group development we find ourselves in, we cast an eye towards the next stage, so we can guide the group to embrace the challenges ahead.

REFLECTION

Think of a group that you are currently actively involved in.
- What stage of group development do you think this group is in now?
    - Write reasons for your assessment.
- Can you remember the group going through previous stages?
    - Jot down some reasons for your assessment of each stage.
- How far ahead would you guess the next stage is?
    - What would you anticipate as some signs that it might be coming soon?
    - How might you help the group to prepare for that shift?
    - How might you help the group meet that shift, when it arrives?

Experiment 19

Facilitating a group to map a shared timeline of their experience

This week's experiment provides a detailed plan for conducting a group discussion on any topic that involves group reflection and achieving a shared understanding. It can be adapted for any topic.
1. For this topic – reflecting on the life of a group over time – choose a group that you are involved in and have a long-term commitment to.
2. Share the five stages of group development with the group.
3. If the group has the energy, organize a time for the group to come together to spend about an hour mapping a 'shared timeline' of the group's life, from its beginning to the present. It may occur at the next meeting or at a later time, depending on the group dynamics.

Here's a detailed process you can use for that future discussion, when it occurs. This is a proven group process for building a shared understanding of any topic.
1. For the 'timeline mapping' discussion, put the five headings up on the wall in chronological order, and give each participant a pad of sticky notes.
2. Introduce the exercise by describing the wall as a 'shared timeline' of the group's most significant experiences, from the past on the left to the future on the right.
3. Describe each of the five stages. Check for understanding.

4. Then, ask them each, quietly on their own, to write seven events in the life of the group that are significant for them personally, and for the group as a whole, putting each event in big writing on a separate sticky note.
5. Then ask each participant to come to the wall and put their note under the stage where they think it belongs. Allow each to do this quietly, in turn.
6. Then ask everyone to gather and mingle at the wall, so they can read one another's contributions. Tell them that, at this stage, they can only ask questions or respond to a question if asked or clarify one another's points.
7. Then ask them to go back to their seats and give them all a different-coloured sticky note. Ask them to put their note on the wall under the stage where they think the group is now.
8. Facilitate a whole-group discussion of any patterns of agreement or disagreement, using the sticky notes to defuse the discussion, for example, 'So these sticky notes are saying this, and these ones over here are saying something different. What do you think that is?.
9. Work with the group to reach as much agreement as possible about where the group is now.
10. Then ask them if they would like to continue the discussion another time and organize that time.

Entry 20: Sustaining groups when things get stuck or conflict arises

By Richard Warner

Small groups, as humble as they may appear, are the heartbeat of community building. They are central to the process because they exist at a human scale, where there is space for *every* person to be included, to connect and to work together. Like any human process, however, groups can get stuck – sometimes *very* stuck.

Anyone who has worked in groups will have had an experience of this: the dominant group member who stifles the contributions of others, the fearful member who avoids sharing their point of view, or two or more members in deep conflict, limiting the possibility of collaboration.

There are many varieties of human 'stuckness'. The good news is that they are all part of the human and group process, and, when approached skilfully, they present opportunities for transformation.

The other bit of good news is that there are time-honoured wisdoms and ways of unsticking the stuckness. We will look at two of these now.

Simple rules and rituals

Simple rules and rituals can provide constant reminders of our preferred way of working together.

One wisdom of working in groups is to establish 'group agreements' for participation early on as a group is forming. These commonly include how we relate to each other, how we make decisions together, and how we manage issues that arise between members. They are best expressed in the language in which they were suggested.

Alongside these agreements go simple rituals we adopt, which embody *how* we want to be together. These should feel appropriate and natural to the group and may include sharing a cup of tea and engaging in social chat prior to a meeting. Some groups have a more formal 'check-in' process for each member, going around to ask how each person is doing or asking, 'What might it take to be present today?'.

Simple rules and rituals also stand 'independent' of any individual, and any individual can call attention to them. The authors have all had the delightful experience of someone else in the group pulling us into line when they see us transgressing!

If you are working in a group and haven't yet laid these foundations, that's not a problem; you could suggest devoting a group session to establishing them.

Surfacing and working through issues

Something many of us find difficult is acknowledging and working through strong differences of opinion and outright conflict. We need to resist the temptation to submerge issues but, rather, surface and work through them as they become apparent, seeing them as opportunities for growth.

Highly skilled group leaders I've noticed will usually raise differences of opinion and potential conflict points early in the group journey, before they become submerged, entrenched, and personalized. Sometimes, it is enough to bring people's attention to differences through storytelling and light humour, allowing them to reflect on these differences and adjust and incorporate them into their worldview.

There are different types of conflict, for example, conflict over values and ideals, personality clashes, and individual behavioural differences. Each will need different processes to be resolved.

And some conflicts are not resolved, but the group can still function by 'managing' the conflict in a way that doesn't submerge it but rather builds safeguards to ensure the conflict doesn't derail the group. One way to do this is to agree to disagree on certain matters and focus on collective efforts towards a shared purpose.

At other times, it might require explicit naming of an issue and structured dialogue between group members to address it. Important in all of this is to act in ways that separate the issue at hand from the personalization of the issue and to view the airing and exploration of differences as a natural human process and an opportunity for transformation.

I have borrowed some ideas about the role of conflict in groups from the peacebuilding and conflict scholar John Paul Lederach. If you are interested in exploring a wonderful method for working with conflict, a great place to start is his *Little Book of Conflict Transformation* (2003).

ENTRY20: SUSTAINING GROUPS THROUGH STUCKNESS OR CONFLICT

REFLECTION

- What ways of relating to each other do you think are important to have as a basis for working with others in a group?
- What rituals have you engaged in that have helped you to connect with others at a human level or have reminded you of the deeper purpose of a group?

Experiment 20

Imagining yourself as an ace group conflict resolver

As Richard says, many of us don't see ourselves as being good at resolving conflict. This experiment asks you to think about yourself in a different way.

1. Reflect on someone in your life who excels at resolving conflict.
   - If you can't think of a particular person, use a situation where conflict was addressed in a healthy way.
   - How did they approach a situation of conflict, and what did they do about it?
   - Describe this person and try to name some steps in their process.
2. Now, imagine you have the skills and understanding of this person, as well as Richard Warner and John Paul Lederach. What would you do differently?

Entry 21: Allowing groups to die well

By Richard Warner

There's a great wisdom expressed beautifully by the late Thich Nhất Hạnh: 'It is not impermanence that makes us suffer. What makes us suffer is wanting things to be permanent when they are not' (Nhất Hạnh, 1999: 132).

We are born into community and, as long as we live, are always connected to it. However, the communities we are part of are always in flux, and it is natural for some to end, or at least for our association with them to.

Endings are just as important as beginnings, and if we manage the transition well, an ending will both honour the work of the group and set members up to form new configurations of community.

Purpose fulfilled, time to move on

Our community enterprise once supported a group of women from refugee backgrounds to form a worker cooperative in a poorer suburb of our large city. They approached us for help because they couldn't find employment and wanted to learn how to create it for themselves.

With minimal assistance, they established and operated a successful community enterprise for several years. After a while, our two organizations lost contact with one another. Some years later, a board member rang to ask me if we would accept a sizable donation from the group, which had now closed and wanted to divest its assets to another charity.

I mentioned how sad I was that the group had folded. She said, to the contrary, that it had been a success, and there was no need for the group now, as all its members had secured ongoing employment. For its members, this group had achieved its purpose, and it was time to move on.

Groups will dissolve for a variety of reasons, from causes both internal and external, but it is often because their initial reason for coming together is no longer as strong as it once was, and their members' energies are required elsewhere. We can sustain the life of a group by incorporating new agendas, energies, and new members.

But there's nothing wrong with them ending. There's also possibly nothing worse than participating in a group where the energy is gone. It can feel like treading water.

So, how do they end well? Mark the occasion, tell stories, and celebrate achievements, and be on the lookout for the ripple effects of that group and where its energies spread next; you may be surprised at the good that comes from letting go.

REFLECTION

Reflect on a group you have been in where the energy became tiring or stale.
- What could have been done to reinvigorate the group?

Or
- How did you successfully mark its completion, or how could you have?

Reflect on a group that you were once a part of that ended.
- What did you learn from this group that you have carried forwards?
- What positive effects did this group spark?
    o Were new connections and relationships formed?
    o Did members go on to do new things?
    o What skills were gained through participating in the group?

Experiment 21

Celebrating the end of a group

Rituals and celebrations are important markers of group endings, providing paths to new beginnings. Think of a group that you have been a part of that ended well or badly.

1. Imagine how you might plan a celebration to mark the end of that group, knowing what you know now.
   - Make your plan as detailed as possible, including who is involved. What, where, when, why, and how?
   - Remember to keep it celebratory, but also to include a pause for the whole group to come together for a more solemn time of ritual.
   - Then, end as heartily as possible.
2. Reflect on how this kind of ending celebration and ritual might have made a difference for the group, and for its members as individuals.
3. Additionally, if appropriate, consider contacting other group members and gathering to discuss this further.

It may also be that you are currently a part of a group that is in the process of ending; if that is the case, you can put this experiment into practice in reality!

Recipe
Caramel slice

Prep time: 30–40 minutes. **Cooking time:** 1 hour. Makes 20 (5 cm × 6 cm slices).

Whether you're a choc-caramel fan or, like me, can't resist the combination of macadamia nuts and caramel, you won't be disappointed by this delightful treat. But you will need to choose. The recipe yields one slice, available in either macadamia *or* chocolate-topped varieties. You could double it, like we do, and make one of each. People ask me for this recipe from time to time, as they can't seem to find one that has the same caramel consistency.

Sisters Carolyn and Susan bake this perfect-every-time caramel slice. And while it has a few steps, it's relatively easy. And like the ladies themselves, the two slices bear a resemblance, but are very different upon encountering. One thing is certain: they both bring a lot of joy (the sisters and the slice)!

INGREDIENTS

Biscuit base

- 250 g of butter
- 2 cups (280 g) of self-raising flour
- 2 cups (180 g) of desiccated coconut
- 1 cup (200 g) of sugar

Caramel filling

- 125 g of unsalted butter
- 1.2 kg (3 x 395 g tins) of condensed milk
- ½ cup (125 ml) of golden syrup

Macadamia topping

- 125 g of macadamia nut halves or pieces

METHOD

Biscuit base

Melt the butter and stir all ingredients together in a bowl. Line a 33 cm × 25 cm × 5 cm rectangle cake tin with baking paper. Add the mixture and spread it evenly over the base of the pan. Then, gently press it until you have an evenly spread biscuit base. Bake for 20 minutes at 170°C/330°F/gas mark 3. It should have an even, lightly browned surface.

Caramel filling

Melt the butter. In a bowl, combine all the ingredients. Pour the mixture over the biscuit base. If you're using macadamia nuts, distribute them fairly evenly and press them lightly into the caramel. (For the chocolate top, leave as is, as the chocolate is added later.) Bake the caramel for 25–30 minutes at 160°C/320°F/gas mark 3 until golden. Allow to cool on the bench, then chill the tray in the fridge for at least 2 hours. At this point, the macadamia slice is ready for cutting and serving.

Chocolate topping

- 60 g of pure cream
- 7 g of unsalted butter
- ½ teaspoon of vanilla bean paste
- 110 g dark melting chocolate

Chocolate top

Once the caramel is cool, melt the cream, vanilla, and butter in a saucepan. Remove the pan from the heat, add the chocolate, and stir constantly until the chocolate has melted and there are no lumps. Pour the chocolate over the remaining caramel slice, then tilt the tray sideways and across to let the chocolate run to all corners, leaving a thin layer over the entire surface. Allow to cool in the fridge for 2 hours before slicing.

Section 6: Interlude. What hinders your involvement in community building?

Over the next few weeks of our journey, Howard Buckley invites us to make conscious and clear the different things that might stop us from trying community building. He examines what hinders us, both personally and relationally, as well as structurally.

Howard gives us the benefit of his hard-earned wisdom and makes himself vulnerable in these reflections, sharing stories of what has hindered him in community building over the many years and decades. Howard invites us to reflect on:

1. **Personal disempowerment** offers some insight into how our relationship with ourselves – our mind, body, and soul – can hinder us or limit our community involvement.
2. **Relational disempowerment** considers the significance of isolation, conflict, and self-interest in our relationships, as well as the challenges of preventing or mitigating their negative impacts, especially in relationships that are key to our community-building efforts.
3. **Structural disempowerment** examines the barriers posed by what we call structures – large systems of decision-making and resource allocation that often overwhelm us and lead us to give up.
4. **The decline of community in the modern world** acknowledges that associational life is in decline; therefore, community building is a tough endeavour and is counter-cultural.

Over these few weeks, we invite you to undertake a series of experiments designed to grow your understanding of yourself as a practitioner of community building and your understanding of your community, exploring some of the barriers to community building that we have found to be most significant in the modern world.

- **Experiment 22. Focusing your community involvement on what energizes you** by identifying those activities that are clear and enthusiastic yeses, and those you might need to walk away from.
- **Experiment 23. Mapping strong, weak, and broken relationships** that are significant to your future efforts to build community.

- **Experiment 24. Understanding your own strategic connections** requires mapping your current connections with the 'powers' in your community – whether government, political, bureaucratic, or corporate – and noting any obvious and easy opportunities to enhance these connections.
- **Experiment 25. Taking a public, pro-community stance** asks you to 'out' yourself in creative ways as 'pro-community', a counter-cultural act in many modern contexts.

Entry 22: Personal disempowerment

By Howard Buckley

When contemplating whether to participate in a community-building opportunity, it is essential to consider our *capacity* to get involved. One way this capacity for involvement can be understood is in terms of our level of power and powerlessness.

Sometimes, the things that prevent us from being involved can seem too overwhelming: we lack energy, we feel disheartened, we experience isolation and even alienation, or we have lost the joy that initially drew us to explore the possibilities of community building.

In such moments, we often feel a sense of powerlessness, and we need to find ways to nourish ourselves, nurture our relationships, and build sustainable connections.

Over the next three entries, a framework for understanding our powerlessness is introduced to assist us in exploring our levels of personal, relational, and structural powerlessness.

Our fluctuating personal capacity for community

This week explores our personal capacity for involvement. When we are feeling physically and emotionally healthy, our knowledge and learning are sound, and our inner wellness is enlivened; we probably consider ourselves in good shape personally to take on the challenges involved in community building. We might say that we feel an adequate level of personal power to be involved.

However, the fragility of these influences can sometimes turn quickly, and our energy, confidence, and commitment can be diminished. This results in community building being one step too far away – it just seems too hard. Too far from the space we are in.

There are many personal reasons why people don't get involved in their communities, and it's not for you or me to judge others on this. But it is important for us to understand what they might be experiencing, and to take stock of what it is that might be preventing or averting our own involvement.

I have lived and worked in places where it seemed for so many residents just too hard to get involved. Their personal circumstances led them to feel disempowered. For some, it was traumas they had experienced, while for others, it was a lack of knowledge or the pressures of raising their families on their own. It could be due to financial capability, or many other complex issues that leave people with little confidence that they could be part of something to make a difference.

Sometimes we get 'stuck'

My own personal power to get involved in community has often been shaken. For me, this can happen when anxiety reduces my capacity to see possibilities and is replaced with a dread that makes me feel stuck.

It is often this 'stuck' feeling that makes it feel too hard to be involved.

Anxiety has many roots, and at times the overwhelming feeling that entraps me is that my efforts are futile and I can't influence change. It's like a shadow of dread has been cast over me.

It's in these times that I have found it necessary to assess what I can and can't do, and focus on where I do have influence and find others to create a shared journey with. I focus my limited energy on what builds more energy.

For me, this has sometimes meant retreating from some activities, so I can focus on activities where I do have influence. After many opportunities to learn this over the years, I now understand that it's okay to say 'no' so that I can say 'yes' to what truly matters to me. These small steps enhance my personal power to contribute to community building.

REFLECTION

- Consider how you feel about your capacity on this journey of community building.
    - o Use a metaphor that's useful to depict that feeling.
- How does it feel to see the feeling in an image or a metaphor?
- Anxiety can sometimes result in 'stuckness'. What kinds of things are likely to get you 'stuck' on this journey of community building?

Experiment 22

Focusing your community involvement on what energizes you

This week, we ask you to do a stocktake of your community involvement, considering the material above.

1. List the community-building activities that you are currently involved in and consider how energized and enlivened you feel about those activities.
    o Which activities are clear and enthusiastic 'yeses'?
    o Reflecting on the wisdom above, what might become 'nos' as this journey into community building unfolds?
    o What will happen if you withdraw from the 'no' activities?
    o How would that make you feel?
2. What barriers do you see to the 'yes' activities, and if these barriers are about your personal capacity, then determine:
    o What can you do to increase your influence in the 'yes' activities?
    o What concrete, practical steps can you take to do this?
        - For example, you might decide to learn a new skill or gain new knowledge, as you are doing with this journal!
3. Would it help to do something that re-energizes you, like going for a walk somewhere you enjoy, immediately before or after the activity?
    o Alternatively, you could make time to read, or prepare yourself, or see a movie the day after or the day before the activity.

Entry 23: Relational disempowerment

By Howard Buckley

We will often feel powerless to act in our community if we do not have strong, healthy relationships. It's hard to get stuff going *alone*, and harder still to keep it going if alone. Let's explore three dimensions of this.

Isolation can limit our opportunities for community

Firstly, there are times when we don't have relationships to start with. Perhaps we're new in a street, neighbourhood, or workplace, or we've become stuck in isolation. I was a stay-at-home dad with our toddler when we moved to a new town to live. We had family support, which was fantastic, but we didn't know others in the community. I was also studying part-time, so I had limited time to build new connections.

I tried attending a playgroup, and I walked our dog during pram walks, but none of these activities led to meaningful connections. It wasn't until a couple of years later that, through our children attending kindergarten and then school, my partner and I formed relationships with others that helped us connect to our community.

Alone, I felt isolated, but in relationships with others, the opportunities opened up for getting involved in my community.

Conflict can impact our ability to work together – if we let it

Secondly, relationships are not easy, especially when conflict, power struggles, or mistrust emerge. At these times, it can seem easier to walk away than to do the work required to sustain relationships. But community building cannot be done alone!

When I became involved in starting a local neighbourhood centre in our town, we formed a committee to establish the organization. All went well until a power struggle emerged, threatening to derail our work together.

There were some who pushed an agenda that sought to exclude others. Some of us felt like leaving, as working collectively seemed like a distant dream. However, we persevered through those challenging times, striving to build relationships founded on listening and graciousness.

We reached a real turning point when we focused on unearthing our shared values: what was important for each and all of us in the kind of neighbourhood centre we wanted to establish. We persevered; we achieved our shared goal of building a neighbourhood centre, and 30 years later, the organization is flourishing.

Community-oriented relationships are counter-cultural

Thirdly, community-oriented relationships are counter-cultural, particularly when the dominant culture in many modern societies is one of competition for individual gain. This is evident in our economic systems and permeates into civil society. We hardly notice it, because we are immersed in it all the time, and it seems so 'natural' and comes so easily to us.

It is all too easy for all of us to dismiss, or simply not notice, other people's attempts to contribute when we can't see past our differences. And, sometimes, we inadvertently focus on our own agendas and ideas, and don't appreciate the potential that other, different ideas might open up.

However, positive relational power is best demonstrated when we consciously resist individualism and competitive behaviour to work together to create change.

Remember, we can't build community; that is, we can't force it to happen. However, we can create an environment in which relationships flourish and community emerges.

Relationships in community building can be likened to the glue that holds communities together. Yet sometimes the glue is not strong enough, or there isn't enough of it. When our all-too-human, fragile relationships fall apart, our efforts at community building are put at risk.

Our greatest strength can quickly be our greatest weakness. We all need to be vigilant. When we see the first hints of isolation, conflict, or 'natural' self-interest in our relationships, those of us who are committed to community need to act to prevent or mitigate the negative impacts that can weaken or break relationships.

REFLECTION

- What are some of the things that prevent you from having the kinds of relationships you desire for community building?
- If you're stuck, what's the smallest thing you can do?
- If you are isolated, what can you do to cope?
- If you are in conflict, what can you do to resolve it?

Experiment 23

Mapping strong, weak, and broken relationships

In this experiment, you will map strong, weak, and broken relationships that are significant to your future efforts to build community.

1. Think about the connections you have and those you would like to build in your community.
2. Draw a 'relationship map' of the relationships you have, or would like to build, with people.
    - Take time to make your map as detailed as you can, with lines that signify the existing connections you have with these people and between them.
    - Use different colours or thicknesses to signify different types of relationships and the strength of the relationship.
    - Find ways to mark those relationships that you can see weakening through isolation, those that are broken or ridden with strife through conflict, and those impacted by the pursuit of self-interest.
3. Use your relationship map to identify up to three key relationships that are at risk of falling apart. How might you strengthen those connections?
4. Identify up to three key relationships that are broken or at risk of breaking through conflict. Identify one small thing you might do to 'nudge' those two people towards the repair of their relationship.

Entry 24: Structural disempowerment

By Howard Buckley

In the previous two weeks, we considered our personal and relational powerlessness. Yet, even when we experience positive inner well-being and strong, energizing connections with others, our power is often diminished by the elements in society over which we have limited control and influence. We call this structural powerlessness.

Structural powerlessness is experienced when organizations act in ways that are dismissive or exclusionary of people or particular groups of people.

Vested interest versus community interest

For example, I remember a time when the local council – a government organization with a fair bit of power – bought a large parcel of land on the outskirts of town, with a view to developing it for community purposes. At the same time, our community had just undergone a local area-planning process, which identified some key social, recreational, and environmental land-use needs desired by residents.

Our assumption was that the council's purchase would be for the purposes outlined in the recent local plan, so it was alarming when instead the council undertook a *new* community consultation, asking what activities could support a new golf course that was to be developed on the newly purchased land.

Many residents were shocked that the council had, behind closed doors, made a deal to create a golf course, which was *not* one of the uses identified as a priority by the community in the recent plan. In response to this community shock and the accompanying uproar, the council established a community taskforce to make a recommendation about how the site could accommodate a golf course and other uses.

Unfortunately, the taskforce was predominantly filled with pro-golf course voices! This process led to the outcome of a golf course being built, and other uses were seen as secondary. Vested interest had won over community interest, and the structural power of the council, in cahoots with vested interests, led to the disempowerment of most of the community!

The ugly practice left many residents feeling that their voices didn't matter. Our concerns were dismissed as those of a 'rabble' – a description often used by those in power, who do not wish to hear or respond to dissent.

Hugh Mackay, one of Australia's most respected social observers, has put forwards a compelling analysis of how many people in Australia have lost trust in the religious, political, civic, educational, and financial institutions. The last two decades have been marked by numerous royal commissions and government enquiries, revealing deep-seated dysfunction within these institutions (Mackay, 2018).

We would argue that this insidious erosion of trust can only be healed by prioritizing community interest over vested interests. We all need to sharpen our ability to distinguish between these vested interests and community interests. Then, we will be able to intentionally and thoughtfully build the strategic connections and alliances that a community needs to enhance community interest and defend it when it comes under threat.

Entrenched social and cultural structures of oppression

Another form of structural powerlessness is the entrenched social and cultural structures of racism, sexism, classism, ageism, and other forms of discrimination in our wider societies, which lead to oppressive practices that keep people separated, impoverished, stereotyped, judged, and sometimes treated cruelly and illegally.

Addressing this type of structural powerlessness requires action at many levels. However, at the community level, we can practise solidarity with those we know in our neighbourhoods who are oppressed, disaffected, and/or alienated, and we can stand together against the discriminatory practices they are facing.

This requires a commitment to justice, as in 'fairness for the most vulnerable', not a community for 'just us'.

REFLECTION

- When you feel disempowered by decisions made by 'powers over', what do you currently do?
- Are there others you can join with to debrief on what has happened?
- Do you know anyone in your community who feels disaffected by a sense of structural powerlessness?
- How can you build resilience with others around you, so that your shared community values might prevail in the face of structural disempowerment or vested interests?

Experiment 24

Understanding your own strategic connections

This experiment builds your structural power.
1. Create a sketch illustrating your current connections with the 'powers that be' in your community.
   - Include everyone you know in government, political, bureaucratic, and corporate roles in, or in relation to, your community.
   - Use different colours or heaviness of line to show the relationships in which you can exert the most influence.
2. Mark any obvious and easy opportunities to enhance these connections.
3. Identify three key influential people whom you do not currently have a connection with, people who you want to have a relationship with and who could support your future community-building efforts. Be mindful of opportunities to meet them.

Entry 25: The decline of community in the modern world

By Howard Buckley

In entry 8, we discussed the importance of social capital as one way of imagining the glue that holds communities together. Now we want to explore how its loss in our society has major ramifications for our work in building community.

We live in difficult times for community

In his book *Bowling Alone* (2000), Robert Putnam identified the benefits of social capital for modern society. He argued that a healthy society is based on a sense of mutual obligation or reciprocity among individuals and groups, and the cooperation of all its parts, while not denying the generative force of conflict. Putnam thought that our greatest need in modern society is for 'bridging' social capital, that is, relationships across difference even while society is in decline.

We witness this decline in the rise of individualism and extremism – groups and individuals closing off from those who are different – and, even worse, marginalizing and vilifying 'others' in ways that destroy social cohesion. As this occurs in a society, growing mistrust and fragmentation make it a very difficult environment in which to build community.

One key way to understand this decline is to recognize the loss of social connections that bring us together and to understand the nature of this loss. For decades, trends have shown that, in modern democracies, we are lonelier than ever. We have shrinking households, increasing relationship breakdowns, and anxiety as a disorder is on the increase. We are more isolated than ever, and despite our new technologies, we report to be more time poor. The modern world discourages people from participating in community life. Yet, healthy community life is part of the solution to our current malaise.

Building bridges with others not like us

So, what is our response? It must begin with building bridges with others who are not like us.

According to the late Australian wise man Michael Leunig, we need to create a new word and become 'xenophiles' – 'lovers of the stranger'.

We need to take risks, to take steps outside our comfort zone, and to embrace differences. We shouldn't try to convince everyone to think like us, act like us, or behave like us. Or, conversely, we shouldn't lose ourselves in others' bubbles of existence. It's more that we need to create spaces where our protective 'force field' can be lowered, and we can allow some of the 'other' into our lives.

Leunig has the last word:

> If you're becoming weary and disillusioned with Australian values [...] or Western civilisation, I recommend strangers – they're such a glorious, redeeming wilderness to wander into. (Leunig, 2006)

ENTRY 25: THE DECLINE OF COMMUNITY IN THE MODERN WORLD

REFLECTION

- Consider the people in your neighbourhood who are strangers to you and ponder why this 'strangeness' might have come to be an accepted and acceptable part of your experience.
- What would it take for you to build a bridge with someone different to you?
- If possible, make a connection with one of these strangers and see what unfolds.

Experiment 25

Taking a public, pro-community stance

What you are doing here in working your way through this journal is already counter-cultural, in the context described above. Here is an idea to take it further.

1. Visit a local T-shirt shop or shop online and purchase a new shirt featuring a pro-community slogan or graphic.
2. Wear it with pride when you go out and about in your chosen community. Notice any looks or comments you get.
3. You might like to extend this with a pro-community bumper sticker or hat, or a pro-community book on your desk at work or on your coffee table at home.

Recipe
Tortilla stack

Prep time: 50 minutes. **Cooking time:** 50 minutes. Serves 8.

This dish is a metaphor for the layers of community that are built over time. Like the Nundah Co-operative, the dish is a mix of things layered to create a satisfying concoction that works. Also, like the Nundah Co-operative, this dish has numerous ingredients and requires multiple utensils.

INGREDIENTS

- 6 large soft flour tortillas
- 1 tablespoon of olive oil
- 1 onion, diced small
- ½ red capsicum (pepper), diced
- 500 g beef mince
- 2 garlic cloves, crushed
- ½ teaspoon of dried oregano
- 1 teaspoon of onion powder
- 2 teaspoons of cumin powder
- 2 teaspoons of paprika
- ½ teaspoon of chilli powder
- ⅛ teaspoon of cayenne pepper (or more if you like it spicy)
- 2 tablespoons of tomato paste
- 400 g can of crushed tomatoes

METHOD

1. Grease and line a round springform cake tin the same size as the tortillas.
2. Dice the onion and capsicum (pepper); keep them separate.
3. Crush the garlic.
4. Measure and combine the dry spices in a small bowl.
5. Drain and rinse the red kidney beans.
6. Preheat the oven to 170°C/330°F/gas mark 4.

Beef and bean mixture

1. Heat the olive oil over a medium heat in a large saucepan.
2. Brown the onion, then add the mince and cook until brown.
3. Add the garlic and dry spices and stir for 1 minute until fragrant.
4. Stir in the tomato paste.
5. Add the water and beef stock powder.
6. Stir in the capsicum (pepper) and crushed tomatoes until combined, and simmer.
7. Once the mixture has reduced (you want it saucy but not too wet or the tortilla stack will be soggy), add the red kidney beans and corn.
8. Taste, then, if necessary, add salt and pepper. Tomatoes can be tart, so we like to add up to a tablespoon of sugar. Stir to combine, and allow the kidney beans to warm through before turning off the heat.

- 1 teaspoon of beef stock powder
- 1 cup (250 ml) of water
- Salt and pepper, to taste
- 1 tablespoon of sugar
- 420 g can of red kidney beans
- 420 g can of corn kernels
- 40 g of unsalted butter
- 40 g of plain flour
- 400 ml of milk
- ½ teaspoon of salt
- ¼ teaspoon of pepper
- ⅛ teaspoon of nutmeg
- 250 g of cheddar cheese, grated
- Sour cream, to serve

White sauce

1. Gently warm the milk in a small saucepan. Do not boil.
2. Melt the butter in a medium saucepan.
3. Add the flour and stir constantly for 1 to 2 minutes to ensure the flour is fully incorporated and cooked.
4. Gradually add small amounts of milk, stirring until fully incorporated in between. Turn off the heat.
5. Season to taste with ½ teaspoon of salt and ⅛ teaspoon each of pepper and freshly grated nutmeg. Remember, you can always put more in, but you can't take it out.

Stack it up

1. Line the base of the springform tin with a tortilla.
2. Spread a ladleful of beef and bean mixture to cover the tortilla.
3. Swirl a little white sauce and sprinkle some grated cheese – it does not need much of either at each layer. A good drizzle and a small handful are enough.
4. Then add another tortilla, layer, and repeat until the beef and bean mixture is used.
5. Finish with a tortilla topped with white sauce and cheese.
6. You may like to put the creation on a tray in the oven to avoid any overflow.
7. Bake for 50 minutes until the cheese is melted and starting to brown.
8. Allow the stack to sit for 10 minutes before opening the springform tin walls.
9. Cut into eight triangles, approximately, and serve with sour cream and a fresh garden salad.

Part 2
Pathways of connecting and change

This part is organized along the themes of ecology, culture, society, politics, disasters, and endings. We would, of course, encourage you to read the endings at the end. But the other themes could be read in any order.

They are ordered in the following sections:

7. Ecological communities
8. Economics as if community matters
9. Community through a social lens
10. Culture and cultural change
11. The politics of people power
12. Endings

Section 7: Ecological communities

In this section, Rachael Donovan takes us on a meandering stroll through her lifetime experiences and more recent experiments and reflections on connecting with the natural environment as a part of our community. Like connecting with human communities, connection in this section means seeing, listening, and deepening your relationship and sense of belonging, and hopefully, responsibility. As Rachael says,

> You may already have a rich relationship with the natural world, or you may feel disconnected or estranged from it. You may even have some fear towards it.
>
> Either way (or anything in between) is completely okay.
>
> There is no right or wrong starting point, and the journey is yours to uniquely explore in ways that are meaningful to you.

Over the coming weeks, Rachael invites us all to connect with the natural world as a living, perceptive, and dynamic part of our community.

1. **Connecting with the natural world** invites us to reweave some of our lost connections with the natural world.
2. **Learning from the natural world** introduces an approach to learning from nature that is open and humble, where we can learn about differences and how to navigate them, as well as the complexity of cohabiting in spaces with diverse needs. Then Rachael focuses on ways our Earth can teach us to deepen our listening.
3. **How to be in a reciprocal relationship with nature** introduces the Australian Indigenous stewardship practice of 'caring for country', which recognizes our deep connection with all beings and the countless gifts nature provides for the lives of generations to come.
4. **Responding to ecological crisis with love** invites you to think about how important love is in all our community-building efforts and ways you can find other people who share your kind of love for the natural world (whatever that may be), then join with them to care for and protect a part of the natural environment, that is precious to you, in your wider community.

Including the natural world in our worldview about our communities can open up new ways of understanding ourselves and our communities. Rachael invites us to experiment with several reflective practices.

- **Experiment 26. Reweaving your connection with the natural world** involves simply going for a walk, noticing how the natural ecology interacts with the human community, and then writing a small, creative piece about one small aspect of your relationship with this local ecology to see it more intimately.
- **Experiment 27. Deepening your listening** introduces a practice for observing the environment with more intimacy than usual next time you spend time in nature, and notice what you can learn about yourself and life through observing the living world in action.
- **Experiment 28. Developing your deep listening skills** helps you identify ways to incorporate a practice of deep listening into your everyday life, as well as the kind of joy, enjoyment, or learning you can expect to gain from these practices.
- **Experiment 29. Finding others who are responding with love** requires identifying individuals who already care for their local environment and are part of groups that share a love for their country that resonates with you.

In our author's collective, Rachael is our very own 'Dirt Girl' (www.dirtgirlworld.com). Her reflections are grounded in her own journey from childhood, giving them depth and resonance for all of us, especially when we can let go of our endless 'adulting' and sense nature as if we were children again. You might like to try it.

You can learn more about Rachael's work at www.threeriversinitiative.com.au

Entry 26: Connecting with the natural world

By Rachael Donovan

There are many ways we connect to nature. The good news is that, as humans, we are already inherently *part of* the natural world, the web of life. Yet, since industrialization, our relationship as a collective has been mostly one of extracting and distancing. Nature is often viewed as a resource we utilize for our benefit.

Growing up with a deep sense of belonging in natural landscapes

While I am also caught in this capitalist-industrial complex, I am fortunate that my relationship to the natural world has always felt strong, close, and rich. Since I was a child, I have felt a deep sense of belonging, healing, and connection in natural landscapes. As someone who grew up in an unstable and often unsafe environment, the natural world became my solace and safety net. Fortunately, being a child of the 80s, I had a lot of freedom to roam and explore on my own. I spent a lot of time wandering through the bushland in my neighbourhood, walking, riding, swimming, exploring, and discovering. I communed with the more-than-human beings through my uninhibited young body, seeing, sensing, touching, and exploring.

As a small child, my mother would take me to Girraween National Park in the Granite Belt region of Queensland, Australia, and it was there that I deepened my connection to *place*. I visited at least yearly as a child and also took my children there regularly throughout their lives. Over time, my connection grew and deepened to one that was not only rich and healing for me, but also more reciprocal and mutual as my understanding deepened. I became part of the place through my love and ongoing relationship to it. Maya Ward, in her book, *The Comfort of Water: A River Pilgrimage*, calls this 'bioregionalism', a philosophy and practice that connects us to place through a deep understanding of its natural characteristics, stories, and cycles.

Pausing to reflect: we cannot love what we do not know

At this point, I'd like to invite you to pause with me and reflect on something Richard Louv says:

> We cannot protect something we do not love; we cannot love what we do not know, and we cannot know what we do not see. Or hear. Or sense. (Louv, 2012: 104)

Please pause and read Louv's words again.

Then look up from this book, and let your eyes rest on the nearest natural feature you see. It might be a tree, a shrub, a mountain, or a cloud. Soften your gaze and gently allow your eyes to observe what is happening there for three long, slow breaths.

Follow this pause into whatever space it takes you. Then continue reading, once you feel your pause is complete.

Living with all the comforts of modernity

Our inherent connection to nature can be easy to forget in modern times, with our climate-controlled houses that protect us from the elements and the wildness and unpredictability of nature (mostly). Being disconnected from this reality comes with a risk and an enormous cost.

The risk is that we cut ourselves off from our own rich, whole, full human selves, as the wild, unencumbered animal beings that we are, deeply woven into this ecological landscape.

And the cost to the planet is evident all around us, as disasters become more frequent and severe, making this cost increasingly urgent and apparent. Ecological and climate collapse is the indirect result of our alienation from the natural world, for as Richard Louv said, we will only love and protect that which we deeply see and belong to.

Our disconnection comes at a deep cost to the planet that sustains us, as well as to ourselves and our communities. Our mental, physical, and spiritual well-being is dependent on a living relationship with the natural world – and our communities that are part of it. And for many of us, this sense of belonging is fragmented, elusive, or not integrated with who we really are.

Reweaving connection with the natural world

But it doesn't have to be this way. Reweaving a connection to the natural world is, in many ways, easier – and certainly less complex – than with the human world.

It can be as simple as pausing for five minutes a day to sit and observe a part of nature, a tree, or a forest. Or to go for a slow, intentional walk, or plant a herb garden.

Even as I write this, I regularly remind myself to pause, pivot, and take a break; to go outside and connect with the living world, and remember my place as an integral, interconnected part of it.

In this small act of resistance and reclamation of my attention in an otherwise busy world, I come home to myself as I feel my nervous system settle and relax. The act is simple, and the rewards are infinite.

REFLECTION

- When you consider the natural world, what do you feel?
    - Is it a part of your daily life?
    - When do you feel part of it?
    - When is it (merely) a resource that you use?
    - When does it feel scary, wild, dangerous, or beautiful (or a combination of them all)?

Experiment 26

Reweaving your connection with the natural world

Identify one small way you can deepen your connection to the natural world this week.
1. Then go for a walk or visit an unexplored natural part of your community or neighbourhood.
2. What do you notice about the natural ecology?
    - What do you notice about the ways it interacts with the human community?
    - What do you observe?
    - What do you feel?
    - What do you need?
    - What does it need from you?
3. Perhaps you could draw or write a poem about one small aspect of your relationship to this local ecology, to see it more intimately.
4. Then, reflect on what you want to do over the next few weeks to reweave your way of connecting with the natural world.

Entry 27: Learning from the natural world

By Rachael Donovan

This week, we take the next step from connecting with the natural world as part of our community to *learning* from it – another aspect of bioregionalism. We learn many things through connection with the diversity of people that make up our communities. If we adopt an open and humble approach, we may expand and challenge our own worldviews and biases. We can learn about differences and how to navigate them. We may learn about the complexity of cohabiting in spaces with different needs, agendas, and ideas. We learn about ourselves through connecting with and listening to others.

This week, we invite you to adopt the same learning approach and extend it beyond the human community to the natural world.

Our Earth can teach us to deepen our listening

The plants and (most) animals have been inhabiting Earth much longer than humans have. This long history of evolution contains deep wisdom and intelligence that has enabled species to survive and thrive. So, we invite you to consider how you can listen to and learn from the other-than-human beings and species in your neighbourhood.

For the last five years, I've lived on Jinibara Country in Maleny, on Australia's Sunshine Coast. Over this time, I have developed intentional practices that connect me to this place beyond being a mere inhabitant, incorporating elements of stewardship, care, connection, and belonging.

I've tried in my own way to practise the process of *dadirri*, or deep listening. *Dadirri* is a term that comes from the Ngangikurungkurr Aboriginal tribe in Australia's Northern Territory. It is a humble way of listening to the land and ourselves, cultivating a quiet inner awareness and stillness. For me, it's a beautiful silence that allows me to connect with life and its many forms.

A month of intimate observation and listening

Recently, I spent a month sitting in the small rainforest on my property for (at least) 30 minutes each day. It was a deep commitment to show up no matter what and listen to and observe both myself and the landscape with the intention of *learning* more about both. As I let the natural world be my mentor and guide, I found myself growing in understanding.

Spending this consistent time sitting and observing deepened my relationship and sense of love and kinship with the land. Through my daily practice, I witnessed relationships between all the beings *and myself*.

Everything seemed acutely aware of everything else, and birds displayed this most obviously, calling and alarming in response to changes and disturbances in the landscape. I observed the reciprocal relationships that sustain life, based on the interplay of receiving *and giving*. Everything appeared to live this dual role: the fungi transform, the insects pollinate, the birds spread seeds, and the trees provide food and shelter.

The polarities of life and death in the environment were ever present. I could see both growth as the expression of life, and decay as the expression of dying – both deeply important to the ecology and often present on the same living being.

I listened to the different calls of the birds and noticed how their behaviour changed based on the quality (or quietness) of my presence. At times, they seemed agitated and called out in alarm; at other times, their call felt like a type of 'check-in' with their companions.

I witnessed a lot of activity, but on the other hand, there were also infinite moments of pause, where things were quiet for a while. There was a quality of both doing and being always at play. Through the listening and observing process, I learned a great deal about myself, including my own resistance and busy mind, as well as the ways I show up (or don't) in my life.

Through this practice of observing the natural world, and myself as *part of it*, I reflected on these ecological wisdoms in my own life. It connected me more deeply to myself and my own journey, allowing me to slow down to the pace of nature, become more attuned to the natural rhythms (both within my body and in the world), and gain clarity on what *truly matters*. This simple practice was profound and transformational. This listening journey is lifelong, and the learnings are vast.

ENTRY 27: LEARNING FROM THE NATURAL WORLD

REFLECTION

- Overall, how do you feel about this idea of learning from the natural world?
- Following the idea of *dadirri*, what might 'listening quietly to country' feel like?
- If you listen to the country you live in, what do you sense?

Experiment 27

Deepening your listening

Next time you spend time in nature – it may be a walk in the park or simply sitting on your back deck – observe the environment with more intimacy than usual.

1. What do you know about the natural features of the place you live – its rivers, hills, soil, and seasons?
   - How did you come to know these things, and what more might you learn?
2. What are the Indigenous names, stories, or histories of the land you live on?
   - In what ways do you honour or engage with them?
3. Notice what you can learn about yourself and life through observing the living world in action. Write it down.
4. Commit to spending some time sitting and observing nature each day this week to learn more about it and yourself.
5. Take some time to observe a natural environment. Make some notes in your journal about how the natural world creates and sustains 'community'.
6. Learn the name of one new plant, bird, or animal species that is native to your region.
   - What is its relationship to the natural community?
   - How does it both give and receive from others in the environment?

Entry 28: How to be in a reciprocal relationship with nature

By Rachael Donovan

The concept of the 'right relationship' is rooted in various Indigenous and spiritual teachings and is based on reciprocal, interconnected ways of relating. From an Australian First Nations perspective, being in the 'right relationship' with the Earth is known as 'caring for country', which recognizes our deep connection with all beings and the countless gifts of clean air, water, food, and medicine they provide.

Caring for country

Also known as 'Earth democracy' (Shiva, 2005), to care for country means to recognize and reciprocate these gifts that we can easily take for granted and to keep the country healthy and strong for our lives, the lives of other beings, and the lives of generations to come.

We probably understand these interconnections intuitively. We recognize that our daily actions have a profound impact on the world around us, but how can we take this instinctive knowledge and apply it more intentionally in our lives? How can we live in purposeful 'right relationships' within our ecological communities?

There are many small ways we can care for country. We could join a local Landcare group or commit to planting a certain number of trees every year to offset our carbon emissions. Growing our own food using sustainable methods is another way to care for the land and become more connected to the ecological systems that support our lives. We can connect with our local First Nations communities and support their practices of caring for country.

Whatever path we choose, just like caring for our important human relationships, caring for country requires us to listen, learn, take time, and pay attention. For me, I usually start by asking, 'What does this place need from me?' And then I take the time to listen and observe what arises.

What does this land want from us?

When we first moved to our one-acre property on the Sunshine Coast, we spent the first year intentionally listening and observing the country without intervening in any major way. We purposely asked, 'What does this land need and want from us?' What do different plants need to thrive and grow? What are the relationships between species (native and non-native)? Who are the other species that inhabit this place we share, and what is our relationship to them? What changes take place over each season?

As we built a deeper relationship with our property through listening and observing its rhythms and patterns, we noticed that this wasn't a one-way process; the beings and land were also getting to know us and were revealing themselves more as trust was built. Birds and animals got used to our presence and treated us with less caution. Our relationships with plants and animals deepened as we spent time getting to know them. We were no longer outsiders looking in: we became part of the ecology.

We began to bridge the human–nature species divide, building a relationship of deep care, reciprocity, and belonging, not dissimilar to our closest human relationships. Through this, we began to see the property differently – more on its own terms. We started to tune in to what it needed from us as custodians, and our role in its ecological well-being.

Sometimes, this meant intervention (for example, heavy pruning or clearing fallen debris); other times, it meant letting the forest and land take care of themselves. Often it was somewhere in the middle. Through observation, we discerned patterns and made informed decisions within the context of the local ecology. It felt like we were working together with the country, rather than us as humans imposing our will onto the land.

Over time, it's become a beautiful 'right relationship' that feels mutually caring and supportive.

ENTRY 28: HOW TO BE IN A RECIPROCAL RELATIONSHIP WITH NATURE

REFLECTION

When considering the 'right relationship', it can be helpful to first identify what it means to you. Let's think about a positive human relationship as an example.

Take a moment and reflect on your closest human relationships. Think about the qualities that make them feel nourishing and fulfilling. As you think of these relationships, contemplate the following questions and note down your reflections.

- Do they listen to what you share?
- Do you feel seen by them?
- Is there a sense of mutuality and reciprocity?
- How are these qualities demonstrated in practice?

Your reflections on these relationships will provide some insight about what the 'right relationship' means to you. The experiment below invites you to now consider these qualities and how you could extend them to the ecological world.

Experiment 28

Growing reciprocity skills

This week's experiment in practice builds on last week's introduction to deep listening. It asks you to harness the qualities you listed above to deepen your reciprocal relationship to the more-than-human world.

1. How does the place where you live care for you – physically, emotionally, or spiritually?
   - How do you care for it in return?
2. Where does your food, water, and energy come from?
   - How might you live in a way that supports local resilience and regeneration?
3. Reflect on your notes from last week and your responses to the reflection questions above. Then write a list of the ways you could bring a practice of reciprocity into your everyday life.
4. Highlight the top three of these practices, the ones you would expect to find most satisfying. Write two or three lines about the kind of joy, enjoyment, or learning that you would expect to get from each of these practices.
5. What is one small thing you can do to continue deep listening with the Earth community?

Entry 29: Responding to ecological crisis with love

By Rachael Donovan

So far in this section, we have explored our connection to the natural world through practices that facilitate listening, observation, and reciprocity, aiming to shift and deepen our personal relationship with the broader Earth community. Part of the wisdom of these practices is that we work collectively for what *we love*.

All revolutionary change has love at its heart

Author and civil rights leader Valarie Kaur (2020) argues that all revolutionary change has love at its heart. Ultimately, love is what motivates people in the long run.

Around the corner from our house is a rainforest reserve, a beautiful 100-acre patch of remnant forest named after environmental activist Mary Cairncross. In 1941, Mary's daughters fought to protect it from loggers and developers, and now it is held in trust, enjoyed and loved by many thousands of people each year.

Peter and I walk through this forest every day, which offers us a beautiful 45-minute retreat from our work-from-home life, dominated by machines and the online world. This forest respite is our sanctuary, a place of connection, life, and care.

Apart from our daily walks, we have spent many hours here engaging in intentional observational practice, both individually and with others, which has deepened our understanding of the forest's rhythms and processes. *We love it*. And it's this love that would make us fight for it if it ever came under threat.

From a community-building perspective, to start by noticing the ecological spaces we love is a great step in responding to ecological crises, particularly if we feel overwhelmed by the scale of the problem.

Working with others to address our environmental concerns

Hopefully, the previous entries have helped you identify and/or deepen your love and care of a natural space in your community. Now it's time to consider how you can *work together with others* to care for and protect it. After all, working with others is what community building is all about.

A group creating a forest reserve is one example. There are many other types. For example, a group might love a creek or beach enough to start a 'clean-up' project, or a native seedling nursery to support the regeneration of a local area. Others might be in love with the idea of a community garden or a renewable energy project.

Ecological challenges can feel overwhelming. Many of us feel very real and understandable emotions of anxiety, rage, and grief in response to the ecological crisis and collapse. In entry 50, we will delve further into working with this sense of despair.

But for now, we invite you to turn towards what you love, for it's in the centre of love that motivation is unlocked. Starting with what we love can help us find the energy to do small things with others, caring for our natural world.

ENTRY 29: RESPONDING TO ECOLOGICAL CRISIS WITH LOVE

REFLECTION

- Do you have an ecological concern you would like to address?
- How and where could you find others who share your concern?
- How much time and energy do you have for this to be a focus at this time of your life? How could you start *really* small?
- How will you find your 'tribe' – the people who you resonate with, who share *your kind of love* for the natural world?

Experiment 29

Finding others who are responding with love

Over the coming days, take a fresh look at your neighbourhood through this ecological lens.
1. Identify individuals who already love their local environment by caring for it.
2. When you've got a good, grounded understanding of what groups are where, make a 'love' map of those places.
    o   Highlight the three where you would expect to feel the most love among the people.
    o   Use a different colour or way to highlight the three that *you* feel the most love for.
3. Stand back from your map and identify the obvious places where you could get involved.
    o   Then, identify where you most *want to* get involved. Is there one that's calling to you, with love?
4. Imagine you are a fly on the wall when this group is having a cup of tea together.
    o   What kinds of things would you want to hear them say about their collective work?
    o   What comments would be red flags?
5. Re-read some previous entries, such as sections 3 and 4, and consider how you want to approach the possibility of more involvement with this group.
6. Then, when you are ready, introduce yourself gently to them. And take it from there...

Recipe
Khulood's falafels

Prep time: 40–50 minutes (plus overnight soak of chickpeas).
Cooking time: 30 minutes.
Makes about 25.

Khulood's journey is a testament to resilience, adaptability, and the power of reinvention. Born and raised in Jordan, she moved to Syria after marriage, but when the civil war broke out in 2014, her family was forced to leave. Seeking stability, they relocated back to Jordan. Determined to equip herself for the future, she enrolled in a range of courses, including plumbing and electrical wiring, as well as sewing and beauty. When Khulood learned that her family would soon be moving to Australia, she signed up for an English language course, eager to embrace her new life in a new country.

Arriving in Australia in 2018, Khulood was determined to build a future for herself and began her studies at a local technical college. In just a few months, Khulood went from not speaking a word of English to holding conversations in it. This rapid progress fuelled her desire to continue her journey of growth and learning.

In 2019, Khulood enrolled in a Kitchen Operations Certificate II run by the Community Living Association in collaboration with Nundah Community Enterprises Co-operative (NCEC). Here, she honed her culinary skills and developed knowledge in food safety. She relished the opportunity to study alongside her friends, forging connections that would last beyond the classroom.

Her practical experience soon followed. In 2021, Khulood and her daughter, Ramia, joined the NCEC as cafe all-rounders for the Good Food Project at the Newmarket Soccer Club Canteen. The pair worked throughout the soccer season, serving the local community with delicious meals. During the off-season, Khulood expanded her experience, taking on cooking roles at Espresso Train in Nundah and Marhaba Café in Brisbane City.

For over four years now, Khulood has been a valued member of the NCEC team. She finds great joy in her work and the sense of community it fosters. Reflecting on her journey, she credits her success to her unwavering determination and the support of those around her. Khulood's story is one of transformation, demonstrating that, with perseverance and an open heart, it's never too late to reinvent oneself and seize new opportunities.

INGREDIENTS

- 250 g of dried chickpeas, soaked overnight
- 1 small brown onion, roughly chopped
- 3 garlic cloves, minced
- 1 cup (60 g) of parsley leaves, chopped
- 1½ teaspoons of ground cumin
- 1½ teaspoons of ground coriander
- ⅛ teaspoon of hot chilli powder (more if desired)
- ¼ teaspoon of bicarbonate of soda
- ½ teaspoon of baking powder
- ½ teaspoon of cracked pepper
- 1½ teaspoons of salt
- For frying, you'll need at least 500 ml of vegetable oil to start; add more if necessary to cover the balls as you fry.

METHOD

1. Soak the chickpeas in a large bowl with enough cold water to cover them completely. Leave to soak overnight, at least 12 hours or up to two days.
2. Drain the chickpeas in a colander.
3. Put the soaked chickpeas, parsley, onion, garlic, cumin, coriander, salt, and pepper in a food processor and blend until the chickpeas are ground to a paste. You may need to scrape down the sides a few times to ensure a smooth finish.
4. Move the falafel mix to a bowl and stir in the baking powder and bicarbonate of soda. Let the mix rest for 10 minutes.
5. Use an ice cream scoop, falafel mould, or moist hands to shape the falafel into balls, slightly smaller than golf balls.
6. Heat the vegetable oil in a deep fryer or pot on the stove to 170°C/338°F.
7. Deep-fry the falafel balls for 5 minutes, or until golden brown. Drain on paper towels.

Section 8: Economics as if community matters

In this section, Richard Warner draws on his experience of managing the social enterprise Nundah Community Enterprises Co-operative (NCEC) to lead us in exploring the relevance of alternative and regenerative economics in community building.

1. **Economics as if people matter** explores the possibilities for maximizing our well-being, with a minimum of consumption. It introduces a local enterprise that is conducting business with a horizon of seven generations into the future.
2. **Finding alternatives within the dominant economy** asks what we can do to counter unregulated growth. Richard offers two ways forwards that we could all contribute to: adopting a regenerative worldview and creating or supporting transformative alternatives.
3. **Transforming the local economy** introduces the concept of 'plugging the leaky bucket' as a tool for envisioning the kinds of economic transformation that would have the greatest impact at the community level.
4. **Alternative economic models,** including the cooperative and mutual enterprise (CME) tradition, and others that are taking off globally.

Richard invites us to experiment with new ways of engaging in our local and wider economies. He challenges us with an old Australian saying: 'put your money where your mouth is'.

- **Experiment 30. Consuming media that promotes community and alternative economics** invites you to find those media sources and add them to your news feed.
- **Experiment 31. Finding local businesses that provide alternatives that are more community-oriented** requires you to review your everyday consumption patterns and support businesses and social enterprises that share your community values.
- **Experiment 32. Starting with the resources you have at hand** invites you to imagine you are starting a new social enterprise, selling something you know nothing about, by using your existing networks and skills.

- **Experiment 33. Moving from consumer to supporter to promoter** asks you to become a member of a local alternative economy group, learn more about it, and then promote it to people you know.

We hope that the reflections and experiments will widen your understanding of how your choices as a consumer can have a cumulative benefit for the community you love.

You can learn more about the NCEC at http://www.ncec.com.au/

Entry 30: Economics as if people matter

By Richard Warner

'Economics as if people matter' is the theme of the groundbreaking book *Small is Beautiful* (1973), written by British economist E.F. Schumacher more than 50 years ago. The book is prescient, describing a modern, 20th-century economy that has made significant strides in creating well-being (for some), yet threatens the very ecological systems upon which life depends. It is recognized as a classic book and has been republished many times. The work of *Small is Beautiful* continues at The Schumacher Institute for Sustainable Systems (n.d.) in Bristol, UK.

Maximizing our well-being, with a minimum of consumption

Schumacher sometimes referred to his perspective as 'Buddhist Economics', a guiding principle of which is to achieve the maximum well-being with the minimum of consumption. He encourages us to consider natural environments not as replenishable resources, but as irreplaceable 'natural capital', that once spent will be gone forever. These are important organizing principles for our modern era, which is beset by multiple and converging environmental crises. To transform these crises skilfully, we will need to employ a different kind of economy than the one that created them.

One of Schumacher's great insights is a *broadening* of the idea of economics, from a narrow lens to one that includes *everything*. In this view, our conceptions of wealth and well-being are expansive, encompassing the flourishing of all people and all the natural systems from which we are not separate.

Conducting business with a horizon of seven generations into the future

This perspective is grounded in Indigenous worldviews. These worldviews have supported environments sustainably for millennia, we will need to listen deeply to them in order to develop a new economics.

An Indigenous social enterprise in Southeast Queensland on Jinibara Country called SevGen has a wonderful way of naming this approach:

> SevGen is short for Seven Generations, which is an Indigenous way of thinking which says that our actions of today will affect seven generations into the future. (SevGen, 2025)

SevGen manages a native 'bush tucker' orchard called Forever Fruits as well as a cafe business, Deadly Espresso, creating employment and training for First Nations people. This type of economic thinking, which considers both people, place, and planet, is one we all need to explore: it is profound, life-giving, and it offers hope.

SevGen is one example of the kind of alternative and transformative economics we will explore in the coming weeks. I am confident you will uncover similar examples in your own part of the world.

REFLECTION

- What are three things you value most?
    - What does being *wealthy* really mean to you?
- What actions can you take to reduce your consumption of materials, but maintain or increase your *wealth*?
- What actions can you take individually and with others to better steward the 'natural capital' and natural systems upon which your future and the future well-being of others depend?

Experiment 30

Consuming media that promotes community and alternative economics

This experiment challenges you to become more mindful of the media you are consuming. Just as you monitor your diet, monitor what you take in from the media, and remember that mass media privileges negative stories and vested economic interests.

1. See if you can find three media sources that give good coverage of local social enterprises, community groups, and alternative or regenerative economics.
2. Add those to your newsfeed so you get more positive stories and learn about alternative sources and suppliers of your everyday needs.

Entry 31: Finding alternatives within the dominant economy

By Richard Warner

Economic practices that power the world's dominant economies are threatening the natural environment, upon which *all* economies rest. Scientific consensus and the wisdom of Indigenous people have been warning us of this for decades. We are now starting to see the impacts in real time, with unseasonal temperatures, the collapse of entire ecosystems, and extreme weather accelerating across the globe.

Unregulated growth is a disaster we can't avoid

All of this is driven by a model of *unregulated growth*, based on the view that humans are somehow magically separate from their environment, and environmental resources are available for exploitation with no downstream consequences.

From my perspective, it's like watching a slow-moving train crash but on a global scale. We know that something must be done to avert the impending disaster, but at the same time, it feels like our individual actions will not make a difference.

The temptation is to avert our gaze, allow ourselves to be caught in a sugar rush of distraction or consumption, or else wallow in a pit of despair. The risk is that we lose hope, and with it any possibility of transformative change.

However, by avoiding these ever-present temptations, we can ask other questions, such as 'How do we live skilfully on the horns of such a dilemma?' and 'How do we spark hope for meaningful collective change?' I'd suggest two ways for us to try.

Adopting a regenerative worldview

The first is to listen to Indigenous peoples and let their wisdom transform your worldview. We will need a new epistemology or 'way of knowing' if we are to transform our economy from one that is extractive, built on the principle of scarcity, to one that is regenerative, based on the principle of gifting and abundance.

Indigenous peoples have rich traditions of sustainable economics honed over millennia – a deep well of transformative wisdom. This wisdom is there for us if only we listen.

In 2024, I was in Santa Fe, New Mexico, and had the privilege of listening to local pueblo leader and food activist Roxanne Swentzell. 'Corn is our mother',

I remember her saying over the kitchen table. This simple phrase is a window into a worldview where plants are not just another resource to be sold and consumed, but rather beings to be respected and circulated.

Recognizing that we are not separate from the Earth we walk on, and its many human and non-human inhabitants, is a gift that Indigenous peoples have to offer, which can transform how we choose to live and how we steward the resources at our disposal.

Creating or supporting transformative alternatives

The second wisdom is to create or support alternatives and not assume that the future is set. Transformative and effective social and economic movements have emerged in the past, often in unpredictable and surprising ways, and will likely continue to do so.

Rebecca Solnit's book *Hope in the Dark* (2016) offers the insight that profound social changes, such as the abolition of slavery and the fall of the Berlin Wall, would have been inconceivable to those living prior to them. The book's subtitle says it all: *Untold Histories, Wild Possibilities*.

Solnit also notes that the seeds of powerful social movements are often initiated by small groups of people acting together on issues that are important to them. The lesson for us is to keep the door of possibility open and continue to walk through it.

As Gandhi once famously said, 'Experiment with the truth'. Nothing is stopping us at this very moment from acting with others on alternatives to harmful patterns of consumption. We can all be involved in building local communities that prepare the ground for future social and economic transformation.

So don't sit back! Find local businesses in your community who are committed to the greater good, and shop there, buy your coffee there, get your taxes done there. Join your local tool library, food cooperative, or urban farming group. No such effort is ever wasted. A connected community is one that is ready and has the capacity to respond in organized ways when the opportunity presents itself. You may be surprised where such action leads and the hope that it fosters.

Amazon Frontlines

A powerful example of hope in action is the organization Amazon Frontlines, cofounded by Indigenous leader Neomonte Nenquimo, whose story is told in *We Will Not Be Saved: A Memoir of Hope and Resistance in the Amazon Rainforest* (2024).

Amazon Frontlines began as a modest initiative aimed at securing clean drinking water for forest communities affected by mining pollutants. It now partners with more than 80 Indigenous communities across the Amazon, protecting land, environment, and culture. They have won legal challenges protecting half a million acres of rainforest. In a time of climate crisis, this benefits all of humanity.

As you can see, there are alternatives to the dominant economy, and many of the best are coming from the fringes. They may be a bit difficult to find, but all of us who are committed to the community can choose to support them.

REFLECTION

- What sparks hope for you? Create a list of individuals and organizations taking positive action in your local economy and explore ways to get involved.
- How many businesses can you name in your community that have an alternative set of goals to the dominant ones? Jot a list, then look it up online and add to the list with new ones that you find.
- What are the *untold histories* of local people exploring *wild possibilities* in your community, city, or state?

Experiment 31

Finding local businesses that provide alternatives that are more community oriented

This experiment asks you to review your everyday consumption patterns and support businesses and social enterprises that share your community's values.

1. If you drink coffee, list the coffee shops in your community, from most community-minded to least. Consider which one you will prioritize for your morning brew.
   - If you like to garden, do the same with garden supplies.
   - If you buy hamburgers, do the same.
   - The same applies to servicing your car or bike.
   - The same for sourcing groceries.
   - You get the idea.
2. What premium are you willing to pay to build a more dynamic community-based economy?
   - Is it 5 per cent, 10 per cent, 15 per cent, or could you even afford 20 per cent?
   - Circle one, off the top of your head! Right now.
3. Then, over the next week or so, compare the prices at the places above.
   - You don't have to shift all your purchasing overnight.
   - Our experience is that we tend to search out these places more and more, because there is a genuine value proposition in being in places and with people whom we like and where we feel most at home.
   - But if you're just getting started, start with one business and see how you like it.

Entry 32: Transforming the local economy

By Richard Warner

One of the most hopeful moments in community building is when people gain control over the poverty they experience (whether material, environmental, or social) and start building a better life. When people act together within their sphere of influence, they can, perhaps for the first time, realize the power they have to transform their circumstances. The magic of this is that what was once a dream becomes a reality.

Sometimes, when we hear about economics, it seems distant, its language foreign, and its levers so far beyond our control that we don't welcome it into our vision of community building. However, communities and the people within them are deeply affected by their economic circumstances and are also significant economic actors themselves. Economics *must* be a part of our consideration in growing healthy communities.

Plugging the leaky bucket

One of the simplest and most powerful tools that can help us to see and influence the local economy is called 'plugging the leaky bucket'. This analogy prompts us to consider the local economy in terms of a leaking bucket.

The 'leaks' are where resources exit the local community, rather than being reinvested and replenished from within. (And for those who have a climate focus, this idea can also be extended to include carbon retention.)

The idea then is to 'plug' some of those leaks, so that more 'wealth' circulates within the local economy, building its health and connectivity and handing back greater control to local people. For example, if we spend money in a bookshop owned by a multinational company, the profits will go elsewhere, the accountants they utilize won't be local, and they probably won't even employ local workers in the local shop.

In contrast, a locally owned bookshop plugs the leaky bucket by employing local people (who spend their pay packet locally), a local accountant or bookkeeper, and the owners (who hopefully make a profit) spend it locally. The knock-on impact of the plugged bucket is that more money flows within the community.

Hepburn Wind Community Co-operative

Hepburn Wind Community Co-operative is an exemplary initiative that has 'plugged the leaks' to foster community ownership of energy production, offering competitive pricing and a reduced environmental impact to a small town in rural Australia.

The project started in the early 2000s with a group of people frustrated at the lack of government action on climate change. Instigating action within the local economy, they developed an investment scheme, raising significant funds from thousands of local people eager to join as members of a new community energy cooperative.

In 2011, a total of AUD$9 m was raised from over 2,000 community investors (about $4,500 on average per investor) to install two large turbines, christened 'Gale' and 'Gusto'. The turbines now power 2,100 homes. Previously, most of the energy used by the local community was generated by a polluting coal-fired power station, and electricity bills were paid to a large corporation with no direct connection to the community.

Now that situation is reversed, with more money (and both literal and figurative energy!) circulating within the local community. New community benefits are emerging, including community education programmes and a bulk purchasing scheme for electric vehicles.

It's just one example of what's possible when people recognize the potential for economic transformation within their local community and take action. Community cooperatives are a great model for circulating resources in local economies.

REFLECTION

- Draw a picture of a bucket, which could stand to represent your street, your workplace, your neighbourhood, or your local community – choose one.
- Reflect on all the resources flowing *out* of that bucket. List them!
- Circle or highlight the top three 'leaks' that you would 'plug', if you could, by substituting a local product or service for one that comes from outside your community.
    - This could be a very humble example; for instance, you might decide that, instead of having a larger company mow the lawn of your unit block, you suggest that the unit owners engage a neighbour who needs a job.
- How could you make those three things happen?
    - What would it take?
    - What role might you play?

Experiment 32

Starting with the resources you have at hand

This experiment is borrowed from the American Zen teacher and social entrepreneur Bernie Glassman (2006), who suggests that we view community economics in terms of preparing a meal using the ingredients we already have to hand.

The challenge is to use your creativity in recognizing, organizing, and incorporating the social and economic resources you already have available to you. Start there!

Like the leaky bucket model, this approach encourages us to see the resources we have within our grasp, and to use them in purposeful ways (however humble that might be) to build community. Its brilliance lies in the simple truth that we don't have to wait for outside assistance to act.

For this experiment, your challenge is to imagine starting a new local enterprise in your community. Just pick something you think you know nothing about, such as selling hiking shoes, for example.

1. Who do you know who might know something about it?
    - How would you approach them?
    - Who else do you know who might know someone who might be good to talk to?
    - How would you organize this introduction?
2. Choosing only from people you already know, who would you want your two key business partners to be? Write their names down.
    - How would you convince them?
3. How will you learn about the thing you are selling?
    - How will you learn what the market might be?

4. Where could you run this new enterprise at the start, until the enterprise can afford to pay rent?
5. How could you promote the enterprise to potential customers, without any money to pay for advertising?
6. Who do you already know who could help you put together a business plan?
7. What else would you need?
    o   How would you access it, using your existing resources and networks?

Entry 33: Alternative economic models

By Richard Warner

Economics is like the air we breathe, touching all that we do. From the humble household budget to those ratified on a national scale, we are profoundly influenced by the resources we have access to and how they are managed. For community builders to ignore the role of economics is to miss powerful ways of building a better world.

As discussed in entry 31, we know that the dominant 'extractive economy' is leading us slowly towards catastrophe. Luckily, there are traditions of alternative economics that offer hope.

The CME movement

Hidden in plain sight is the CME movement. It arose in response to deep inequalities of the industrial revolution of the 1800s and was developed by people seeking a way out of poverty. The solution they presented was that *ordinary people could organize equitably* to achieve scale and economic power.

Because there was a need and the model worked, CMEs quickly spread to all areas of the economy. 'Friendly societies', for example, were once the only way to access sickness benefits, and trading cooperatives were the only way people could compete with wealthy individuals to bring their goods to market. CMEs were also the first businesses to insist on a level playing field regardless of gender, background, or personal wealth.

CMEs have been phenomenally successful and are now a global movement. It might surprise you to know that more than 1 billion people – one-eighth of the world's population – are members.

The Self-Employed Women's Association

An inspirational modern CME is the Self-Employed Women's Association (SEWA) of India. Founded in the 1970s by global elder Ella Bhatt, SEWA supports the independence of more than 2 million women experiencing poverty working in the informal economy (SEWA, n.d.). They help women cooperate on issues relating to their economic exclusion and have made significant inroads to ending their poverty. From humble origins, SEWA now has a member-owned bank, childcare services, and a university. They are a political force to be reckoned with.

The CME movement demonstrates that a good economic idea at the right time can profoundly change people's lives, and this is just one model for community builders to explore. Others include:

- **Social enterprises** that trade like any other business but exist specifically to make the world a better place. You will find local, state, and national associations in your part of the world.
- **Local exchange trading systems (LETS) schemes**, also called local employment and trading systems or local energy transfer systems in different parts of the world. LETS are locally initiated, democratically organized, not-for-profit community enterprises that provide a platform for members to exchange goods and services, using a locally created 'currency'.
- **Circular economy** movements around the world aim to prevent materials from becoming waste and to regenerate nature. In a circular economy, products and materials are kept in circulation through processes such as maintenance, reuse, refurbishment, remanufacturing, recycling, and composting.
- **B Corps** are businesses linked in a non-profit network whose aim is to transform the global economy to benefit all people, communities, and the planet. Their motto is 'We won't stop until all business is a force for good' (B Lab, n.d.).
- **The gift economy** is an economic system based on gift giving, in which goods or services are exchanged without expectation of remuneration, reciprocity, or repayment.

What's important is not a particular model, but the development of an economic literacy that helps us to see beyond the prevailing orthodoxy and envision new, inclusive, and sustainable ways of producing and sharing wealth.

REFLECTION

- What alternatives to traditional economics are you already involved in? Make a list: you might be surprised by your level of engagement.
- Look up online your locality's name plus each of the following terms: cooperative, mutual, community enterprise, social enterprise, LETS, circular economy, B Corps, gift economy. See what you can find hidden in plain sight in your own suburb, town, or city.
    - o Are you surprised?
- What area of your life and the life of your community could be improved through changed economic practices?
    - o From saving on the cost of living, to generating employment, or retaining services within the local community, list some areas where you think change needs to occur, for the greater good of the wider community, in your small part of the world.
- What alternative economic practices would you like to explore?
    - o What will you dip your toes into, and experiment with, in this coming year?

Experiment 33

Moving from consumer to supporter to promoter

This experiment requires you to act! It won't take you too much out of your way, and trust us – it will be fun.

1. Find one alternative economic organization you can engage with in your community, starting as a customer, supporter, or member.
   - For example, you could join a tool library or repair cafe, or shop for some of your food at a local veggie cooperative.
2. Become a member and start using it for yourself.
3. Then, make deeper connections within the organization, so you understand how it works in practice.
4. Then start to promote it. For example, you might offer to invite friends and family to check it out with you, or you might offer to volunteer to support the activity or distribute a promotional flyer in your neighbourhood or workplace.

Recipe
Gardener's pie

Lentil cottage pie. Vegan and gluten free.
Prep time: 30 minutes. **Cooking time:** 1 hour 20 minutes. Serves 6.

This is a great meal to share because, being gluten free and vegan, almost anyone can eat it (there are always exceptions, like Howard, who can't eat legumes). Not only does this comforting dish have great flavour, but it's also familiar (in its traditional form) to most folks.

At Espresso Train Cafe, we often ask Danny to peel and chop the vegetables. Danny is a founding member of the NCEC. He helped form the Co-operative in 1998 and has worked in every aspect of it. Since starting modestly in the grass-cutting team with a push mower (and summer chaff, they tell me), the team gradually expanded the contracts and acquired commercial equipment, including ride-on mowers.

One morning in 2012, Danny got out of bed as usual but collapsed to the floor, unable to walk. Doctors discovered a large tumour near his spine, and, after surgery, he could not regain the use of his legs. Danny has adapted to life in a wheelchair, and the Co-operative has adapted jobs to suit Danny. These days, Danny not only prepares food at Marhaba Cafe but also works in our greenhouse, where he establishes small plants and repots large ones for our landscaping contracts. He's also planning to raise herbs from seed to use at the cafes. From horticulture to hospitality, the Nundah Co-operative strives to balance participation and production!

INGREDIENTS

- 2 tablespoons of olive oil
- 1 brown onion, finely diced
- 1 large carrot, finely diced
- 2 sticks of celery, finely diced
- 2 garlic cloves, crushed
- 250 g brown lentils (dry)
- 200 g red lentils (dry)
- 1 litre of water

METHOD

1. Heat the oil in a large pot over a medium heat and cook the onion, carrot, and celery for 5–6 minutes, until soft and translucent.
2. Add the garlic to the vegetable mixture and cook for a further minute.
3. Add the brown and red lentils, water, and vegetable stock powder. Cook for 8–10 minutes until you can squash a lentil between your fingers.
4. Add the tomato paste, crushed tomatoes, Italian herbs, and pepper. Reduce until the sauce has thickened (about 30–40 minutes).
5. Taste for seasoning. If necessary, add salt and pepper to taste.

- 1 teaspoon of vegetable stock powder
- 2 tablespoons of tomato paste
- 400 ml of crushed tomatoes
- 1 teaspoon of ground black pepper
- 2 teaspoons of Italian herbs
- 1 cup (150 g) of frozen peas
- 1 cup (150 g) frozen corn
- 1 large sweet potato
- 2 or 3 large potatoes
- 2 tablespoons vegan 'butter'
- Salt and pepper, to taste

6. Stir through the frozen corn and peas. Continue to cook for 5 minutes, then set aside.
7. Meanwhile, peel (optional) and cube the sweet potato and potatoes. Preheat the oven to 180°C/356°F/gas mark 4.
8. Put the sweet potatoes and potatoes in a large pot, then cover with salted water. Bring to the boil and then simmer rapidly for 20 minutes until tender.
9. Drain, and then mash in a bowl with the vegan butter, salt, and pepper.
10. Grease a deep 25 cm pie dish. Pour the lentil mixture into the dish until it is two-thirds full. Top with the mixed potato mash. Bake until lightly browned (about 30 minutes).

Section 9: Community through a social lens

In this section, we examine community through a social lens, guided by two of our authors' collective, Rachael Donovan and Dave Andrews.

Rachael revisits her formative experiences with the CREATE Foundation and takes us into her recent work with people experiencing homelessness, reflecting on her experiences with asset-focused, peer-to-peer community building within communities of interest. She leads us through reflections and experiments on two topics:

1. **What are the social assets in your community?** This includes those that might surprise us with their resilience and capacity for community leadership.
2. **The pandemic of social isolation: looking out for the lonely**, through a community-building approach.

Dave is typically challenging, indeed sometimes confronting, in his two passionate reflections:

3. **Exclusion, inclusion, and solidarity** for Dave means that the challenge of inclusion is deeply personal, and none of us can dodge it. If we are going to weave truly inclusive communities, *we* (you and I both) need to find ways to include those whom *we* often exclude.
4. **Identity as a vehicle for division or connection.** In this reflection on the fault lines of social division – often around class, race, gender, disability, and sexuality – Dave focuses on the importance of remembering what unites us and the challenge of developing inclusive identities.

To guide our efforts in building community through a social lens, this section includes four experiments.

- **Experiment 34. Mapping your community's assets**, as a tool for identifying and building strategic relationships.
- **Experiment 35. Building community connections** by initiating a conversation, then creating a connections map, and sharing your thoughts, in a lightly held dialogue.
- **Experiment 36. Invite someone you normally wouldn't to have a cup of tea (or something) with you,** 'then think through what it would take to invite more of these marginalized 'others' into spaces

where you are comfortable, but where they could make you or others uncomfortable.
- **Experiment 37. Building your own more inclusive identity** that better reflects who you are becoming or aspiring to be.

This is a challenging section. It challenges us to step out of our comfort zones and engage with people we currently avoid. Enjoy!

Entry 34: What are the social assets in your community?

By Rachael Donovan

A 'social asset' is any social resource that improves the quality of a community. These resources are made up of:
- individual people's strengths, passions, and gifts; and
- the strong and flourishing connections, relationships, and networks within each community.

These could include local organizations and groups, such as parent–teacher associations, local charities, educational groups, environmental groups, and special needs organizations.

When we think of community building, it's beneficial to start by leveraging these social assets. Then we start with what already exists and build on what's already strong (see entry 4). Communities can then create a foundation of resilience and self-reliance, addressing issues and concerns from within, rather than waiting for or relying on external solutions.

We should also remember that even the most marginalized or economically disadvantaged communities possess a range of social assets.

A good service does not make a good life

However, the modern focus on what is sometimes called a 'service approach' to solving social issues can end up ignoring, and thereby eroding, the social assets within communities. Within this approach, citizens are seen as clients or consumers rather than active and valuable participants in community life.

Within the service approach, professionals are often perceived as the 'experts' who bring solutions to local challenges, which can erode confidence in local knowledge and experience. While we all need good and reliable services, as Cormac Russell says, a good service does not make a good life (Russell, 2020). But participation in a strong community does.

What contributes to a good life is built from the community and its social assets. The trick as a community builder is to look in new ways, so that we can identify these resources that already exist. This is also good wisdom for professionals to consider: how to not bring solutions but be catalysts for social assets to be mobilized and strengthened in a street, neighbourhood, or workplace.

Street Up: lived experience leaders in homelessness

Like many parts of the world, homelessness on the Sunshine Coast, Australia, has become a growing concern in the community. Over the last few years, the local government has been looking for new and innovative ways to address this challenge and has noticed that people with first-hand experience of homelessness have not been included in the conversation. That is, a key social asset was missing when attempting to address the problem.

While appropriate services are a crucial component of addressing homelessness, which encompass support, resources, and accommodation, the council recognized that the voices of those who have experienced homelessness are a crucial asset in understanding the problem.

With the support of other community builders, the council decided to be a catalyst for mobilizing social assets around this concern. They worked with a few local neighbourhood centres to identify and invite people with lived experience of homelessness to come together and discuss this issue. From this, a group was formed based on their ideas, passions, skills, and strengths. Over time, the group Street Up was born.

Street Up is a group of eight Lived Experience Leaders and other partners, working to raise awareness about homelessness, reduce stigma, and help support effective, compassionate, and inclusive responses.

Through Street Up, social assets in the community that were previously hidden – that is, people who've experienced homelessness – are being harnessed and activated, and together these Lived Experience Leaders work with others to contribute to change.

ENTRY 34: WHAT ARE THE SOCIAL ASSETS IN YOUR COMMUNITY?

REFLECTION

- What are your own personal assets that you bring to building a thriving community?
- Think of your gifts, skills, passions, knowledge, and experience. Make a list, ask others, and keep adding to it over the coming weeks and months.
- What is already strong in your community? Write a list and keep adding to it as you notice more things over the coming weeks and months.

Experiment 34

Mapping your community's assets

This week, you are going to build a map of social assets in your wider community. In the same way you wouldn't go to the supermarket without first checking the cupboard, asset mapping enables us to identify existing strengths, skills, and gifts in the community.

The purpose of this map isn't simply to gather data for its own sake, but it's about identifying and building strategic relationships, recognizing that we can't know what we need until we know what we already have.

You might want to work with others to create a social asset map. It might be helpful to draw it on an actual map of your community. On the following page, sketch a simple conceptual map of your broader community. Then add notes and graphics in response to these questions:

1. What do people care about in this community, and what is already being done collectively to address it?
2. Where are people gathering?
3. Are these groups or individuals connected to one another?
4. If not, could they be? How?
5. How strong are the existing relationships between these groups and individuals?
6. How could they be strengthened?
7. Identify a few of these people or groups that you'd like to connect with for a cup of tea, with the purpose of building new connections and learning more about what is already strong in your community.

Entry 35: The pandemic of social isolation: looking out for the lonely

By Rachael Donovan

As discussed last week, strong social assets are what enable communities to thrive. Assets signify what a community already has: its strengths in people, relationships, groups, and organizations.

The challenges of isolation and loneliness for our communities

This week, we consider how social assets can help address the growing challenges of isolation and loneliness faced by people in many communities.

While isolation and loneliness have been a growing concern for decades, since the COVID pandemic, rates of social isolation and loneliness have increased, and it is now estimated that one in four people around the world are affected (World Health Organization, 2023). The World Health Organization identifies that people who lack social connection face a higher risk of death, increased rates of anxiety, depression, and dementia, and increased risk of cardiovascular disease and stroke. It has become a significant public health concern worldwide, affecting individuals of all ages.

Many organizations attempt to address the issue of social isolation by devising a solution. They might 'come into' a street or neighbourhood to 'set up a group' or 'organize an event'. This is the service approach discussed last week. In contrast, here are two stories of a community-building approach.

A community-building approach to social isolation

As a young person who spent time in out-of-home care, I felt very isolated and disconnected. It felt like everyone else had a family and 'normal' homes, an anchor that connected them to the world. It was a very difficult time, and, being young, I didn't have the skills or resources to build my own healthy connections.

As I shared in entry 6, it was by good fortune that I was linked to an organization, the CREATE Foundation, which was made up of other young people in out-of-home care. In this experience, I was seen as an asset (not a 'delinquent' or through a deficit lens) and was invited to participate in the work of the organization with all my strengths.

Through this experience, I found a place among peers; I was listened to and valued, and I was connected to others who wanted to make a difference. This organization helped uncover and build upon the gifts of young people who faced many life challenges, enabling them to feel included and participate in the community in meaningful ways.

Benarrawa Community Development Association

Another organization that has been working to build community using their own organization as a social asset is Benarrawa Community Development Association, a community centre in Brisbane, Australia.

Since 2021, it has been intentionally connecting with community members who may be experiencing social isolation or loneliness. They recognized that people experiencing isolation might not feel confident or comfortable accessing their community centre, so they knocked on doors and listened to people's experiences to build connections and break down isolation.

Over time, as relationships developed and trust grew, members of the community were invited to the centre to connect and meet with others, and to share cups of tea and stories. Through the process, people's gifts, knowledge, and skills were recognized, and much laughter was shared.

The social asset of the community organization was used to facilitate a safe space where connections were formed and friendships developed. The organization didn't create a group but instead activated social networks.

These stories highlight the wonderful work that many organizations are doing in our communities to address social isolation and loneliness. But, as community members, we also have a role to play in building social assets to address isolation.

REFLECTION

- Take some time to reflect on the unique gifts you have that could contribute to building connections in your community.
    - Do you have a skill that you could share?
    - Are you a great networker?
    - Can you run an amazing event?
    - Are you highly empathetic and a great listener?
    - Do you have lots of spare time and want to be more involved?
    - Do you love meeting people?
- In what ways do you already bring these gifts to your community?
- Reflect on a time when you felt lonely or isolated. What types of connections would have made the difference for you during this time?

Experiment 35

Building community connections

This week, we invite you to initiate a conversation that will unfold gently over the coming weeks.

1. Start by discussing the issue of loneliness or isolation in your neighbourhood with someone else. Listen for insights they offer that you would not have immediately thought of. Keep it light.
2. When you have time and space at home, sit with the space below or a piece of paper and identify the types of people who may be impacted by isolation (examples could be seniors, newcomers, or people living alone, but be aware of assumptions, and don't limit yourself to these groups).
3. Perhaps consider chatting with your local community centre to see what they are already doing.
4. On the other hand, identify individuals in the community who are well resourced and connected, and who may be interested in contributing to building community connections. These people are true social assets, already well connected and networked.
5. Create a 'connections map'. Identify the gaps.
6. Reach out to two or three well-connected individuals and share your thoughts. See if it is a shared concern, remembering to hold your 'agenda' lightly.
7. See what emerges. If it is shared, discuss some ways you can start to address what you have in common together by building connections or engaging with networks in the community.

Entry 36: Exclusion, inclusion, and solidarity

By Dave Andrews

Even when we are part of social groups that are more inclusive of others, each group we are a part of typically prioritizes its own individual and collective self-interest over that of others.

Defying the conventional wisdom of our times

A conventional norm is to 'look after number one'. So, we all tend to 'put ourselves first, and others last'. Where we are concerned for others, we usually put those we consider strong, intelligent, interesting, beautiful, rich, or famous people 'first', and those we consider weak, ignorant, boring, ugly, poor, or unimportant people 'last'.

After all, the convention is we want to relate to those who will return our investment in them. And who better to return our investment in them with interest than strong, intelligent, interesting, beautiful, rich, and perhaps even famous people?

Where we are concerned for those that we consider weak, ignorant, boring, ugly, poor, or unimportant, we tend to put the ones that we feel 'hopeful' about 'first', and the ones that we feel 'hopeless' about 'last'.

After all, if we are going to go out of our way to help people, we want our attempts to be demonstrably effective and make us feel successful. So, we tend to avoid helping the people we consider 'no hopers'. They are some of the 'last' people we have in mind.

The challenge of inclusion is deeply personal, and none of us can dodge it

If we are going to weave truly inclusive communities, we need to find ways to include those whom *we* often exclude. And we all have our own preferences.

However, to reweave marginalized people into our communities requires a radical commitment to 'put the first last, and the last first'. This means we need to make a conscious decision to act contrary to the conventional attitude of our society by considering 'most', those who most consider 'least'. As such, we should invest our time, our energy, and our money in the lives of people whom we cannot expect to repay us but who, unexpectedly, often do.

And we should pour ourselves into relationships that fail as often as they succeed. These are the relationships that never fail in helping us become the more authentically loving human communities that we aspire to be.

Reaching out to the very people whom most people consider least

When my wife, Ange, and I moved into our locality, we made a commitment to prioritize paying attention to those who are often overlooked.

As we got to know the neighbourhood, we noticed there were groups of isolated people with disabilities living in hostels. A hostel owner who attended our church invited us to drop in at teatime to get to know the residents. They told us they'd love to go out, so we began taking them to local parks to play football and have barbeques together.

Over time, we became such close friends that, when our daughter got married, they all attended the wedding, and many were part of the wedding party! When our adopted Nepali daughter was attacked, it was our friends from the hostel who ran to her rescue and saved her from serious assault.

The threads of relationships we'd woven together had become solidarity, and that solidarity had become a safety net for us all.

REFLECTION

- How do our conventional attitudes lead to unintended marginalization?
- Why are people reluctant to get involved with those who are *most* marginalized?
- Why is it important to 'put the first last, and the last first' to be truly inclusive?
- What can you learn and put into practice from Dave and Ange's story?

Experiment 36

Invite someone you normally wouldn't to have a cup of tea (or something) with you

This experiment challenges you to consider what steps you could take to include some people who have often been excluded from community activities where you are very comfortable.

1. Identify three 'types' of people in your community whom you and others consider 'least'.
2. Think through your networks. Who do you know who has a connection with one of these people? In Dave and Ange's story above, they learned that one of the local hostels was run by a woman who attended their local church.
3. Think carefully about how you would approach just one of these people to get to know them.
4. Do it.
5. Then, when *they* are ready, and this may take a few meetings for each of you to discern the other's trustworthiness, gently invite them to join you for a cup of tea or coffee at a place you are comfortable and familiar with.
6. Reflect on how that goes, what you want to do next, and how you can make it more comfortable for both of you. Start by reflecting on any surprising moments of mutuality or solidarity, particularly noticing if and how they were initiated by the other person.
7. What would it take to expand on this, and invite more of these marginalized others into spaces where you are comfortable, but who would make you and other people uncomfortable?

Entry 37: Identity as a vehicle for division or connection

By Dave Andrews

In seeking to weave and reweave the threads of our relationships with others, the only place we can start is from ourselves.

Our sense of self as people in relation to others is what we often refer to as our 'identity'. Much of our 'identity' is a 'gift', which includes the ethnicity, family, education, religion, aptitudes, and experiences we have been given. However, much of our 'identity' can be chosen by ourselves, like our choice of occupation, musical appreciation, and political affiliation.

When I reflect on my own 'identity', I am aware I am a white Anglo-Australian cisgendered heterosexual male who has been married for 50 years with two children and four grandchildren.

I have been nurtured in a Christian tradition, educated in postgraduate community development, and worked in relief, rehabilitation, and development in Australia and Asia.

I've enjoyed living in India, savouring cups of tea, indulging in kebabs and naan, listening to soul, blues, and melodic rock, and recording my own folk-rock songs. I've also enjoyed reading and writing books on spirituality and community, as well as playing and watching tennis and football (go Matildas!).

Identity as a way of being seen

Our 'identity' is a way of being seen as individuals and as members of social groups. In fact, while 'identity' may be individual, it is never merely a matter of personal preference. 'Identity' is not only about how I recognize myself, but also about how others recognize me.

'Identity' is always collective in nature and, as such, is a social phenomenon. I am never just seen as an individual, but as a person representative of a group with which I am seen to have a shared 'identity'.

Our 'identity' is not only a way that we are seen by others, but also a way we see others. If we identify our humanity too much with our religion, politics, culture, class, gender, or sexual orientation, we will not be able to see our common humanity with others.

Building inclusive identities

A big part of the collective work of building inclusive communities is the individual work of building inclusive identities and sharing them with others.

In 2017, an Australian TV advertisement for meat caused a furore by depicting Ganesha, the beloved elephant-headed Indian god, having a chat with other people over a plate of lamb. Australia's Indian community was in an uproar, as Ganesha (and many Hindu people) are vegetarian.

An Indian friend asked me to join his community in a protest at Parliament House. I publicly supported these Hindus, Buddhists, and Jains who have a sacred tradition of *ahimsa* (not eating meat). The *Brisbane Indian Times* newspaper reported that 'Dave Andrews, a Christian, and a meat-eater supported the protest'. I was seen not merely as 'Dave Andrews', but as a 'Christian' and a 'meat-eater' (Andrews, 2021: 99).

Being seen as the 'other' is often not helpful. But, in this case, being seen as the 'other' was helpful as it showed a community that 'others' were committed to a common cause.

To weave community, it is important to remember what unites us through developing inclusive 'identities', for example, as 'all Aussies', or through developing multiple identities, which can help us connect with distinctly different groups of people through shared human interests, like music, sports, culture, or the arts.

ENTRY 37: IDENTITY AS A VEHICLE FOR DIVISION OR CONNECTION

REFLECTION

- How would you describe your own identity?
- What parts of your identity are exclusive to you and make you unique?
- What parts of your identity are inclusive and can provide links to other people?
- Who are some types of people in your community whom you could develop connections with by exploring shared human interests?
- What are some steps you could take to develop those connections?

Experiment 37

Building your own more inclusive identity

In this experiment, we will work with what unites us by experimenting with the development of inclusive 'identities' that better reflect who we are becoming or aspire to be.

1. Revisit your reflections above.
   - You might want to discard some of your identities – that you are tired of, or that no longer serve you or who you are becoming.
   - Now would be a good time.
   - Just put a fat line through them and bid them a grateful farewell.
2. List the top five or 10 identities you have that you really value about yourself, and your potential to contribute to the world in ways that are important to you.
3. Consider how you can express each of these identities in a more inclusive manner.
4. Finally, craft your own new identity statement, using language that is inclusive and respectful.
   - It might help to start each new statement with 'we' rather than 'I'.
   - Then imagine standing with others who are also affirming the statement for themselves, so that you and they are saying it simultaneously, collectively.
   - Imagine this is happening at a kind of 'coming out' – a public gathering of your community.
   - How does your new identity stand up to this test?

Recipe
Vietnamese-style rice paper rolls

Prep time: 40 minutes. **Cooking time:** 0 minutes.
Fun time: unlimited. Serves 2–3.

When presenting to friends for lunch or dinner, I call these 'making your own fun rolls'. They are a good icebreaker meal as you need to pass around the ingredients. They are doubly good because they work for almost all dietary requirements (even Howard's!). Just put everything out in bowls and make yours just how you like it. They have been a staple on the Espresso Train Catering menu for over a decade, not only because they're easy to make, but because they're also healthy and delicious. Of course, for catering, we roll them up ready for guests to dip and enjoy!

INGREDIENTS

- Rice paper (available at supermarkets or Asian grocers)
- ¼ pack of thin vermicelli noodles, softened (see directions on packet)
- Protein like prawns, chicken, or pork, cooked or cold
- Vegetables
    - carrot, julienne
    - cucumber, julienne
    - capsicum (pepper), julienne
    - bean sprouts (optional)
    - avocado (optional)
- Herbs
    - coriander leaves
    - mint leaves

METHOD

1. Thinly slice (julienne) all the vegetables into matchstick-sized pieces.
2. Pick the leaves from the herbs and compost the stems.
3. Combine the dipping sauce ingredients.
4. Fill a large bowl with warm water.
5. Put everything on the table. You may want to add other sauces, such as hoisin, chilli, or soy.
6. When ready to roll, soften the rice paper in the bowl of warm water. You can add more than one at a time but ensure the first one is fully submerged before adding another. Don't add more than you are going to make immediately. Once soft (about 30 seconds) remove the first one first, and so on. Spread the rice paper on a plate, then put small amounts of your favourite fillings in the middle. Fold one edge over the filling and roll, bringing the sides up as you complete the roll. Dip or drizzle with your favourite sauce and devour fresh.

Alternatively, if you want to make them ahead:

1. Toss the noodles in a large bowl with the julienne vegetables, chopped herbs, and a little dipping sauce. Taste.

Vietnamese dipping sauce (or store bought, but be careful of dietary requirements)

- 2 tablespoons of caster sugar
- ¼ cup (60 ml) of hot water
- 2 tablespoons of lime juice
- 1 tablespoon of rice vinegar
- 2 crushed garlic cloves
- 3 tablespoons of sweet chilli sauce (again, careful of dietary requirements)
- 1 tablespoon of fish sauce (omit if you have vegans or seafood allergies)

2. Continue making rolls until all the filling is used up. Serve with more dipping sauce on the side.
3. Keep covered in the refrigerator for no more than 10 hours, as they will dry out.

Section 10: Culture and cultural change

In this section, Dave Andrews reflects on a lifetime of building community in diverse cultural contexts. Dave has lived in India, Afghanistan, and West End in inner Brisbane. He has worked in Christian churches, adult education institutes, and in deep theological dialogue with colleagues in Islamic and other faiths. He has been a prominent author-activist in campaigns for social justice, asylum seekers, and the local impacts of encroaching gentrification.

He invites us to reflect with him on the 'glue' of culture in building community:

1. **Cultivating a culture for community** asks us to focus on how we can initiate and maintain community activities that foster a sense of significance and solidarity among diverse participants.
2. **The role of the arts in community** looks at how we can utilize creative expression to facilitate diverse conversations that foster community.
3. **Culture creators, not just consumers** looks at ways that enable us to initiate a wide range of community initiatives and create an environment in which others are doing the same.
4. **A culture of creative resistance** uses creative processes, like 'guerrilla theatre' – disruptive political performances in public places – as an effective form of radical protest that aligns strongly with values of non-violence and creativity.
5. **A community of cultural diversity** presents a fundamental challenge in our efforts to build community, while also providing important opportunities as a creative catalyst for cultivating a sense of solidarity.

Many people, including the authors themselves, have journeyed with Dave in the experiences he describes, learning from his thoughtful, passionate, and deeply held commitment to a creative and compassionate form of community that actively and intentionally embraces people on the margins.

If you resonate with Dave's approach, you may want to visit www.daveandrews.com.au and explore his numerous books on related topics.

This month, we invite you to participate in five experiments that will help you incorporate a cultural component into your practice.

- **Experiment 38. Sharing a meal with friends** is a way of developing your consciousness and sensitivity to community culture.
- **Experiment 39. Playing with a creative 'third object'**, to enhance your understanding of any community, at any time.
- **Experiment 40. Becoming a creative contributor** to an existing community group.
- **Experiment 41. Imagining your own kind of creative guerrilla theatre** by 'holding' a community concern lightly in your imagination and looking at it from a different angle every day for five or six days.
- **Experiment 42. Exploring community connections and cultural diversity**, identifying connections that you most want to strengthen, and 'natural' connections that might provide an invitation.

These will hopefully shift you into active engagement with some of the key challenges and opportunities of culture in community.

Entry 38: Cultivating a culture for community

By Dave Andrews

In *Basic Communities*, David Clark reminds us that:

> Community [is] essentially a sentiment which people have about themselves in relation to themselves: a sense of significance and a sense of solidarity. (Clark, 1975: 4–5)

In order to create community, we need to cultivate a 'culture' that creates 'a sense of significance and sense of solidarity' in our locality.

A 'culture' is simply 'a way of life': a way of eating and drinking, a way of speaking and listening, a way of working and relaxing, a way of commemorating and celebrating our life together. It is contained in the advice that we give one another about good and bad manners, how we greet strangers and how we meet and make friends, and so on.

To cultivate or reclaim a culture that creates 'a sense of significance and sense of solidarity' in our locality, we need to (re)encourage a safe, accepting, and respectful way of life, which makes people feel welcome, included, and involved in our community.

In many societies throughout history, people have intentionally cultivated this kind of culture, often through traditions of hospitable ways of eating and drinking together.

The West End shared meal

One of the most interesting and enduring experiments I have been involved in was a shared meal that deliberately included lonely and alienated people in our inner Brisbane neighbourhood of West End.

As we got to know people living on the margins, we asked what they wanted and what would help them feel a real part of our community. We learned from them that one of their priorities was having a meal together with others from their neighbourhood. So, we decided to start what we called a 'community meal'.

From the beginning, the community meal was a shared experience. In fact, some people referred to the 'community meal' as the 'share meal'. The term implied that the meal was not a 'welfare' event, where others provide for us, but a 'friendship' event, where we provided for one another. Those who had a lot were encouraged to bring a lot. Those who had a little were encouraged to bring a little. But everybody was encouraged to bring something along for the meal.

Some people used to bring casseroles in crockpots. Others would bring what they would be eating anyway: hot chips from their favourite charcoal chicken shop, or maybe a few tea bags or a small milk carton.

When there were just a few of us, we used to meet at someone's house, but as time went on, word got out, and the number of people who dropped in for dinner grew, so we had to move into a community centre.

Over the next 20 years, up to 50 people gathered regularly, every fortnight on a Friday night. It was a party to which everyone was welcome, no matter how badly dressed or badly distressed. It became a party for everyone in the area who was left off everyone else's party list, including some of the most fragile and some of the most freaked-out characters in the city. In time, we became friends. We shared not only the latest local gossip but also some of the deepest parts of ourselves, along with some of the previously best-kept secrets of our lives.

REFLECTION

- Why is cultivating culture so crucial for creating community?
- What aspects of community culture are most important to you?
- How do hospitable ways of eating and drinking together cultivate a culture of community?
- How could you embody a safer, accepting, and respectful way of daily life?

Experiment 38

Sharing a meal with friends, paying attention to culture

1. Have a meal with some friends in your community.
2. Notice the many ways that eating and drinking together cultivate a culture of community.
3. Imagine ways that this group could open itself up to include more marginalized people in the community, through their existing natural connections.
4. If the group did this, what attitudes might need careful attention, to preserve a core attitude of 'friendship', and prevent an unconscious shift to a 'welfare' mentality?

Entry 39: The role of the arts in community

By Dave Andrews

The arts include a wide range of human practices that involve creative expression. They encompass multiple diverse modes of thinking, feeling, being, and doing through a broad range of media. Arts such as storytelling, singing, dancing, painting, sculpting, drawing, writing, performing, and filmmaking are modes of creative expression that help us cultivate a sense of significance and a sense of solidarity, which are intrinsic to our sense of community.

Arts like writing, drawing, painting, and modelling can provide a safe way of expressing ourselves, externalizing our internal world of ideas and attitudes. We can reflect on what the object of art reveals about our solidarity with ourselves and/or others. Then, based on what we now understand, we can address the issues that are raised.

Using a third object in community building

An object of art, sometimes referred to as a 'third object', can provide a focus for a group of people meeting tentatively together, taking the focus off themselves or each other, and putting it on a poem, a song, or an object. We have used all of these to diffuse uncomfortable tension and facilitate unexpected levels of deep individual and collective reflection. It can be an amazing, disarming way of cultivating a sense of significance and solidarity in a group.

Storytelling is one of our most ancient and yet one of our most powerful creative acts. It is primitive as it precedes the use of tools; it only requires a person who is willing to tell a story. It is powerful because the stories we tell ourselves shape our lives, challenging our minds, engaging our emotions, and enchanting our imaginations.

Bill the barber and rock 'n' roll George

Let me tell you a story that illustrates the role of the arts in community. It starts with Bill, the barber in our neighbourhood. Bill has a single chair in his barbershop. He refused to expand his business, wanting it to stay a small, humble, human enterprise.

When Bill is not working, he paints. Bill is Greek Orthodox and typically paints iconography. One day, rock 'n' roll George asked Bill if he would paint a picture of him standing beside his beloved FJ Holden car. Bill painted a full-sized portrait. Rock 'n' roll George loved it. So did the community. It celebrated rock 'n' roll George, who lived with an intellectual disability, as the local legend he was. The painting was proudly displayed in the Queensland Art Gallery adjacent to our neighbourhood.

A Greek man who owned the fruit and veggie shop next door to Bill's barber shop saw the portrait and asked Bill if he would paint a picture of rock 'n' roll George for him, too. After all, rock 'n' roll George came into his shop looking for bargains nearly every day. Bill said he'd paint him a portrait on one condition: that the owner of the fruit and veggie shop would give rock 'n' roll George free fruit and veggies for the rest of his life. It was agreed. Bill painted the portrait, gave it to the shopkeeper, and rock 'n' roll George got free fruit and veggies for the rest of his life.

ENTRY 39: THE ROLE OF THE ARTS IN COMMUNITY

REFLECTION

- What do you think about the role of the arts in building community?
- What are the arts that cultivate a culture for community in your locality?
- What are some of the lessons you can learn from the story of Bill the barber?
- What can you do to encourage the use of the arts to cultivate a culture of community?

Experiment 39

Playing with a creative 'third object', to enhance your understanding of any community, at any time

Your job this week is to see if you can find a creative 'third object' that is from, expresses, or speaks to a part of your community that you would like more insight into.

1. Bring it home with you, or a photo of it.
2. Sit with that object and write down as many insights as you can about the nature of that part of your community. Go for a walk; clear your head.
3. Repeat step 2.
4. Repeat step 2 again.
5. Reflect on the progression across these three rounds of creative observation.
    - What do you learn about what you want from your community?
    - And what does your community want from you?

Entry 40: Culture creators, not just consumers

By Dave Andrews

A capitalist economy can reduce many of us to the role of mere consumers. If we want to cultivate a culture that creates community, we need to recover our role as creators.

For the last 40 years or so, I've been involved with active networks of people, working together to build a better community where I live in West End, intentionally focused on creating spaces for people on the margins.

One of our simple experiments included hosting reading groups in our homes. People enjoyed sharing books on the intersections of spirituality, social justice, and community.

GROW group: a good anchor for an inclusive, creative culture

One group that became central to our efforts was our own local GROW group. GROW is an Australian, national, 12-step, do-it-yourself, self-help, peer-support group focused on participants' mental health and well-being. GROW is anonymous and inclusive: it is open to all people, regardless of colour, class, or creed, who respect the group and would like to participate in order to enhance the mental and emotional health of our society.

Our GROW group was open to a wide range of participants, including some with diagnoses and others without; some were medicated, while others were not. It provided a common ground. As we say in GROW, 'May the spirit of friendship make us free and whole persons, and gentle builders of a free and whole community' (GROW, 2025).

Creative spin-offs initiated by a diversity of creative community builders

These activities were complemented by groups experimenting with non-violent communication and conflict transformation, sharing backyard spaces to create permaculture gardens, organizing fruit and vegetable cooperatives, and helping each other brew homemade beer. Another activity some people engaged in was dumpster diving: scavenging discarded, high-quality food from supermarket bins, which was prepared and shared as healthy, hearty meals with people on the streets.

Over the last 40 years, as we have gradually gained experience and expertise, people have been able to create more complex community organizations. Some of us created a community association as an officially recognized, legally registered, formal organization that multiple community groups use as an auspice for their community experiments.

Others of us created the Community Praxis Co-op to strengthen the capacities of other groups and organizations through professional community development projects, consultation, training, and mentoring. And others created a non-profit community company to make solar power accessible to everyone in an ethical and affordable way, using high-quality, low-cost solar panels and batteries.

Many people in these networks have chosen part-time employment, allowing us to have the time and energy to commit to creative community ventures. We also discovered that choosing to live close to one another in a locality developed a rich, dense, multifaceted, relational neighbourhood-level base. Together, we created a kind of 'compost' from which creative initiatives seemed to sprout like mushrooms, and which supported them to grow and thrive.

REFLECTION

- Which of these creative initiatives do you relate to most?
- How do these creative initiatives foster a culture of community?
- What is the biggest challenge for you in resisting being reduced to the role of a consumer?
- How can you best exercise your own agency in the role of a creator of community?

Experiment 40

Becoming a creative contributor

This week, we invite you to identify an existing grassroots group that is running successfully and where you would like to become a participant.

Commit for four months and, over time, notice any shift within you from 'space to place to base' and in your capacity to become a creative contributor to the group (remember entry 1).

1. Month 1: as you get a feel for how the group works and how you might contribute, make a conscious shift from 'consumer' to 'creator of culture' within the group. Notice how you go about that, what works for you, what doesn't, and the nature of any resistance you encounter.
2. Month 2: look for other creative culture creators in the group. They will not necessarily be the leaders. Can you see existing 'creative synergies' among the more creative people in the group? How can you initiate connections or accept invitations that create space for people's creativity?
3. Month 3: how might you build momentum from within the group towards a creative and compassionate form of community that actively and intentionally embraces people on the margins? What are the limits of this within that group?
4. Month 4: when will you need to start something new to take this further? Who will your 'we' be – the 0–1–3 comrades with whom you share deep cultural values, and that can create a kind of 'base'? (Remember section 5.)

ENTRY 40: CULTURE CREATORS, NOT JUST CONSUMERS

Note that, if you take on too much responsibility in the group too soon, you will not have the space or energy to make this experiment your focus. There will be plenty of time for all of that later, if you decide to stick with the group.

Entry 41: A culture of creative resistance

By Dave Andrews

The arts provide a range of possibilities for our own creative resistance to oppression.

In my community-building work across various settings, my colleagues and I have found 'guerrilla theatre' – a term specifically coined to describe disruptive political performances in public places – to be an effective form of radical protest that aligns strongly with our values of non-violence and creativity.

Campaigning against state-sanctioned child abuse

By 2015, many people in our community had become frustrated with trying to change the federal government refugee policy, which we argued amounted to 'state-sanctioned child abuse'. So, we decided to call for social and economic non-cooperation with government agencies and boycotts of and strikes in detention centres. We also called for political non-cooperation through open civil disobedience, refusing to cooperate with unjust government regulations.

On 11 October 2015, doctors at the Royal Children's Hospital refused to discharge asylum-seeker children back into detention. Doctors at the hospital were concerned about the welfare of dozens of patients and said it would be unethical to discharge them to unsafe conditions that could compromise their health (Hatch et al., 2015).

In early February 2016, one-year-old 'Baby Asha' was treated at Lady Cilento Children's Hospital after she was injured in an immigration centre on Nauru Island. Asha's injuries healed, but doctors refused official demands to discharge her, upon which she would be returned to detention on Nauru, saying it was not a safe place for the baby.

The child's fate focused the attention of Australians who were concerned about the government's treatment of children of families seeking asylum.

The federal president of the Australian Medical Association called for people to support the doctors and nurses at Lady Cilento Hospital, which was just around the corner from us. So, on 13 February, we joined protesters rallying at the hospital in support of the doctors and nurses.

Guerrilla theatre in action: a candlelight vigil to mobilize support

On 17 February, we hosted a candlelight vigil at Lady Cilento Hospital called 'Light the Dark', to demonstrate our support for the Let Them Stay campaign for Baby Asha, her parents, and the nearly 300 mums, dads, and children who were being threatened with removal to Nauru, and also for the brave doctors, nurses, and other staff who were risking their careers to defy federal directives, in order to protect Baby Asha.

On 20 February, hundreds of protesters surrounded exit points at the hospital amid reports that there were plans to move Asha and her family to immigration detention. We stopped police cars coming out of the hospital on the Saturday night to check that the child was not inside. The group was good-natured and showed no aggression (ABC, 2016).

Finally, on 22 February, Baby Asha was released from Lady Cilento Hospital into community detention, with the government's assurance that she was not being moved to Nauru Island.

ENTRY 41: A CULTURE OF CREATIVE RESISTANCE

REFLECTION

- How and why do you think 'guerrilla theatre' works?
- What did you like about these disruptive public performances?
- What did you learn that you could use, if necessary, to protest injustice in your community?

Experiment 41

Imagining your own kind of guerrilla theatre

This week, we invite you to think creatively about a concern you have for an issue in your community that seems intractable, or simply 'stuck'.

Imagine some creative ways that a group of citizens who share your concern and might become your friends and compatriots could draw the attention of the wider community to this concern.

The practice of 'imagining' is like the practice of 'loitering with intent' we discussed in entry 10, only it occurs entirely in your mind.

1. Just 'hold' the concern lightly in your imagination and try looking at it from a different angle every day for the next five or six days.
2. Each day, jot some notes about the possibilities for creative action, including guerrilla theatre, that occur to you, and leave each to 'ripen' – or not – while you add others.
3. Allow yourself to muse gently about what it would take to actually do it.
   - What kinds of allies or compatriots would you need to have?
   - How might it be misunderstood by your community?
   - How might it be misconstrued by your 'opponents' – those advocating for the opposite case – in your community?
   - How might it play out, depending on the weather, or if done at a different time of day or on a different day of the week?

Musing like this allows your ideas to ripen and mature, which is essential if you are going to follow through with them, because you will inevitably face obstacles and probably will encounter opposition.

While this experiment is conducted solo, you can also imagine adapting this process collectively as a triad, with two other committed and creative allies. We have found it useful to work with artists and other people who are naturally creative.

You might even want to shift it from imagined to actual!

Entry 42: A community of cultural diversity

By Dave Andrews

Cultural diversity can sometimes present challenges in our efforts to build community, due to racism, discrimination, and many other forms of exclusion, yet it also provides important opportunities as a creative catalyst for cultivating a sense of significance and solidarity.

My home, Australia, is known as a multicultural country, uniting a multitude of cultures, from the 500 languages of the First Australians to the newest arrivals from more than 300 different cultural backgrounds.

The challenge of a deeply divisive cultural event

Each year, 'Australia Day' confronts all Australians with the challenge of recognizing and engaging with the cultural diversity in our country (Reconciliation Australia, n.d.)

We are confronted by the fact that, while many non-Indigenous people celebrate 26 January as 'Australia Day' and remember it as the beginning of European settlement of Australia, most Indigenous people commemorate 26 January as 'Invasion Day' and remember it as the beginning of the European colonization, dispossession, and expropriation of their land.

My involvement in my own multicultural inner-city Brisbane community West End presents its own challenges. Each morning on 26 January, I usually join First Nations friends at the 'Invasion Day' rally in Brisbane that begins outside Parliament House, proceeds through the city, stops for speeches and chants, crosses Victoria Bridge, and then ends in Musgrave Park, near where I live.

But sometimes supporting a 'blackfella' protest against 'whitefella' oppression can be complicated. One year, I turned up carrying the 'Always Was, Always Will Be Aboriginal Land' banner, and was publicly singled out by Aunty Jean, an Indigenous elder I know well from church circles. In front of a very angry mob of 'blackfellas', she asked me, a 'whitefella', to pray for everybody before we started.

I didn't know what to do. I certainly didn't want to show disrespect to Aunty Jean or cause her to lose face in any way. If I didn't do what Aunty Jean asked, it could prove I was a 'conceited white bastard'. But if I did do what Aunty Jean asked and prayed for the assembled mob of 'blackfellas', it could prove I was a 'condescending white bastard'.

I decided to do what Aunty Jean asked. I said a prayer for the protest, doing my 'whitefella' best to voice the heartfelt cries of all the 'blackfellas' who were gathered. When I opened my eyes, I was gratified to see fists raised in a Black power salute.

The challenge of hospitality to our migrant communities

In the afternoon, I had organized a street barbecue for neighbours, many of them first-generation migrants from England, Ireland, Greece, India, and the Philippines.

It didn't seem unrealistic. Most of us sent our children to the same school and used to turn up at the same school nights, where children from more than 50 different countries would bring the house down by singing 'I Still Call Australia Home'.

But when I had asked a Greek neighbour, Spiro, if we could have the barbecue in the street in front of his house, while he was happy to comply, he said he wouldn't come himself.

'Why won't you come, Theo?' I asked him, using the common honorific for 'uncle'. His reply left me stumped: 'If I bring my wife, she feels left out. If they hear her speak in Greek, they say, "Speak in English!". When I say she doesn't speak much English, they tell us, "Go back to Greece!"'. I said, 'We are your neighbours; none of us will treat you like that. This is your street; you have the right to speak your language in your street. And my wife, who is Greek, would be happy to speak to your wife in Greek.' But it was not enough. He didn't come.

It'll take more effort before all the people in our street can 'Still Call Australia Home'.

REFLECTION

- What can this story tell us about relating to Indigenous people in our own part of the world?
- What lessons can we learn about relating to migrant people?
- What are some celebrations that are culturally contentious in your community?
- What are the strongest celebrations of cultural diversity in your community?
    - o Is there a way you can strengthen them, or their impact on people you know?

Experiment 42

Exploring community connections and cultural diversity

This week, we invite you to apply the knowledge you have gained over the past month to explore your current understanding of cultural diversity, connections, and tensions within your broader community.

1. Using a creative medium of your choice, draw a representation of your existing community connections in terms of cultural diversity.
   - Use a variety of colours and leave ample space around the outside of your drawing.
   - Then, overlay the dynamics of cross-cultural expression that you are aware of, across and among these people.
   - Then add what you know about the dynamics of cross-cultural tension.
2. Then, around the outside, add in cultural groups you are *aware of* but *have no connection with*, in your community.
   - Then add individuals you know who belong to those groups.
3. Go for a walk. Then stand back and look at your drawing. What does it reveal?
4. Identify three connections that you most want to strengthen. Highlight them.
   - Then, stand back again and look for 'natural' connections that might provide an invitation or support your connection with those people.

Recipe
Lamb toshka with Marhaba house salad

Prep time: 20–30 minutes. Cooking time: 10 minutes. Serves 8.

Lamb toshka is a dish inspired by Zyad, who worked tirelessly with our Marhaba Cafe team in its first year and a half. Zyad is a Syrian refugee who is over 60 years old, is always hard at work, always cheerfully singing in Arabic, and is an avid tea drinker. One day in the kitchen, Zyad cut his finger on a mandolin slicer. While we were tending to the injury, we commented to him on how bad it was. Zyad said that it was not a bad injury, then showed us a scar as long as his upper body along his side and around his back where he had been hit by a rocket during the war. So, compared to a rocket, I guess a cut on the finger is not so bad at all. Working alongside these wonderful humans helps provide a bigger perspective and reminds me how lucky I am.

INGREDIENTS

Lamb filling

(Note that you can cheat by substituting the below dry ingredients for 1 heaped tablespoon of curry powder)
- 750 g of lamb mince
- 1 garlic clove
- ½ teaspoon of ground fenugreek
- ½ teaspoon of cumin
- ⅓ teaspoon of ground cloves
- ⅓ teaspoon of ginger
- ⅓ teaspoon of cardamom
- ⅓ teaspoon of cinnamon
- ⅓ teaspoon of curry powder

METHOD

Make the lamb filling

1. Start by measuring all the dry ingredients into a small bowl. Stir to combine.
2. Heat a small amount of vegetable oil in a deep, heavy-based pan over a medium–high heat. Add the lamb mince, breaking it up into small pieces to avoid any lumps. Stir until browned.
3. Add the garlic and dry ingredients to the mince and stir for 1 minute until fragrant.
4. Add the tomato paste and pomegranate molasses. Stir until the liquid is absorbed.
5. Add salt and pepper to taste. The mixture should be caramelized and not wet.
6. Set aside to cool (now is a good time to make the garnish and sauce).
7. Once cool, add the grated halloumi cheese and stir until well combined.

- ½ tablespoon of sweet paprika
- ⅓ cup (80 g) of nigella seeds (optional)
- 1 tablespoon of tomato paste
- 1 tablespoon of pomegranate molasses
- 1 teaspoon of salt
- ½ teaspoon of cracked pepper
- 180 g of halloumi, grated (or your preferred cheese)

Marhaba Cafe house salad

- 700 g of mixed lettuce leaves, washed and spun dry
- 1 punnet of cherry tomatoes, halved
- Half a Lebanese cucumber, cubed
- 1 or 2 raw baby beets, very finely sliced
- Half a red onion, sliced thin (optional: pickle the onion in a mixture of white vinegar, a pinch of salt, and a teaspoon of sugar. Toss and leave to pickle while cooking the lamb filling).
- Pickled chilli or cucumbers
- Pomegranate molasses
- Chewy cranberries and toasted almonds (see the Aleppo Chicken topping in section 2)
- Yoghurt sauce (see the Aleppo Chicken recipe in section 2)

Assemble the toshka

1. Spoon 120 g of the lamb and cheese mixture onto one half of a pita and spread.
2. Fold the pita in half to make a semicircle. Lightly press together.
3. Gently grill the folded pita in a pan, turning to toast both sides (or toast in a sandwich press) until crisp and the filling is warmed through. Cut into three triangles (pizza-shaped) from the centre of the straight side.

Make the salad and serve

1. Make salad by gently tossing the leaves, tomato, cucumber, and red onion together.
2. Place big handfuls of the salad mixture on each plate.
3. Drizzle with pomegranate molasses.
4. Rest the lamb toshka on top of the salad.
5. Drizzle the entire dish with yoghurt sauce.
6. Top with cranberry and almond garnish and a sliced pickled cucumber or chilli.

To serve

- 8 pita flatbreads or similar

Section 11: The politics of people power

Over the next few weeks, Dave Andrews reflects on a lifetime as a prominent author-activist in campaigns for social justice, asylum seekers, and the local impacts of encroaching gentrification.

Dave invites us to reflect with him on his somewhat unconventional and profoundly radical approach to thinking about power and politics. Sometimes, power is framed in opposition to love. Love versus power. In contrast, Dave inhabits a politics of love where true power is filled with love.

1. **Personal, relational, and structural power** revisits the framework introduced by Howard earlier, with a focus on how we can free up our own 'agency' to better embody a 'politics of love'. This approach focuses on people, not parties, emphasizing policies that empower the disempowered, and strongly opposes injustice done to the disadvantaged, but also strenuously practises respect for all, including our opponents.
2. **Traditional power and transformative people power** argues that we need to discard the traditional approach and embrace a transformational approach to political power. This involves growing our own individual and collective agency. By paying attention to the ways we use power with one another and within our groups, we can develop a power that is strong yet gentle – a power that essentially comes from within an individual or a group of people.
3. **Subverting dominating institutions** introduces a very 'Dave' way of working for change indirectly rather than directly, so we don't immediately threaten the hierarchies, structures, ideologies, and entrenched cultures of dominating institutions. All his co-authors recognize Dave as a master of this practice.
4. **Forming alliances to counter the politics of division** reflects on Dave's many years of experience of interfaith dialogue, practising the politics of love by not only cooperating with 'friends', but also finding new ways to collaborate with those who are becoming dehumanized and even demonized as 'enemies' in the public commentary of political aspirants in our communities.

There's no way of getting away from the capillary nature of power. It's pervasive and everywhere, in all relationships: intimate, personal, and transactional. Power, of course, plays out in systems and structures, and is therefore institutional and organizational. From our perspective and experience, Dave has one of the more honest and self-reflective approaches to power. He has always tried to advocate for and embody a 'power-with' approach and self-control, rather than a 'power-over' approach by controlling others. We hope you find his approach as challenging and insightful as we have over the years.

This month, we invite you to engage in four experiments:

- **Experiment 43. Stepping into your own power** gives you a structured experiment that you can adapt to any topic at any time in the future. In it, you get grounded and centred and take a small step towards who you would like to become, every day for six days.
- **Experiment 44. Inviting change** is an experiment in shifting from controlling someone else to controlling yourself. It is a basic reflective practice, which can also be adapted to any topic at a future time, reflecting on how *you need to be different* in order to *invite another person* into the kind of ongoing relationship that can bring transformative change to both of you, and to your networks, and eventually to your wider community.
- **Experiment 45. Creating cracks in resistant institutions** is an imaginal practice, asking you to revisit the same topic every day for at least three days, with the intention of becoming more creative each time.
- **Experiment 46. Build a bridge and get over it** challenges you (and all of us) to identify when our own inner prejudices quietly subvert our best intentions. Often, the best thing we can do is build a bridge to the people we are 'othering' and find a way to join them in their own world.

We hope these experiences enable you to step into a more open and collaborative relationship with others in the community, rather than walking away from issues of power, conflict, and resistance.

Entry 43: Personal, relational, and structural power

By Dave Andrews

Politics is about power. Power is about agency. Agency is the ability to act.

In our communities, there are three levels at which we can express our power: the personal level (in ourselves); the relational level; (with others); and the structural level (as part of a group).

Politics is about the way we express our power in groups and exercise our power as groups to utilize our resources and solve our problems.

We often feel powerless. Powerlessness is the inability to act.

For example, at a personal level, I often get depressed. I feel like I'm a nobody and there's nothing I can do. At a relational level, I often get discouraged. I fear that no one likes me, so I withdraw from relationships, and I can't get involved with others. At a structural level, I often feel like I'm just a small cog in a big machine. I can't change anything that really matters.

Although we may *feel* powerless, we are not entirely powerless.

Recovering our agency and ability to act

Whenever I am tempted to feel powerless, I intentionally seek ways to regain my personal, relational, and structural power.

At a personal level, each day when I wake up, I spend some time contemplating the simple truth that I am not nobody, I am somebody. I can't do many things, but I can do some things. And, of the few things I can do, the things that I think are 'right' and feel will be 'good' for the community are the things I will do.

At a relational level, most days I spend time developing my relationships with people in my community, those who are 'good' people and who want to do 'good' things in the community, regardless of their age, gender, culture, or religion. Starting with my extended family, I reach out through my personal networks in the area to build the kind of relationships I value, with anyone and everyone I can.

At a structural level, I regularly participate in informal groups and formal organizations dealing with political issues in our community. Most of these secular and religious groups and organizations were already established in my community when I moved in, and I am happy to support these 'good' people, who are doing 'good' things in the community. I occasionally step in and out of informal 'leadership' roles in these groups, when I can see a particular contribution I can make. But I rarely take on formal leadership roles.

Love Makes A Way

Where necessary, I have helped start groups. One example of the more explicitly political of these is Love Makes A Way (n.d.), which tries to better embody a 'politics of love' that focuses on people, not parties; emphasizes policies that empower the disempowered; and strongly opposes injustice done to the disadvantaged, but also strenuously practises respect for all, including our opponents. There is more on this in entry 44.

As a final reflection, consider the following.

Each of us who feels inadequate needs to remember our capacity to act, and each of us who feels afraid needs to realize our courage to act.

Each of us who feels stuck needs to remember the potential of our actions, and each of us who feels insignificant needs to recognize the importance of our actions.

Every act of truth is a victory over deceit. Every act of love is a victory over hatred. Every act of kindness is a victory over violence.

Every risk a person takes to stand up for justice and peace with grace is a victory in our strong yet gentle struggle to make our dream of a healthy community a reality (Andrews, 2017: 33–34).

ENTRY 43: PERSONAL, RELATIONAL, AND STRUCTURAL POWER

REFLECTION

- How would you describe your relationship with politics?
- What would you say is distinctive about the 'politics of love'?
- Which of the challenges in the last paragraph resonates with you?

Experiment 43

Stepping into your own power

This week, we give you a structured experiment that you can adapt to any topic at any time in the future.

1. Reflect on your own sense of powerlessness.
   - Does it feel predominantly personal, relational, or structural?
   - Which of these would you most like to strengthen or grow?
   - What is the gentlest way you can imagine doing this?
2. Create a quick image or representation of the slightly more powerful version of yourself that you would like to become.
3. Place it somewhere it can stay for the next six days, with 3 m or so in front of it.
   - Turn your back on it, and take three paces, then turn around to face it again. Keep it in your field of vision, with 'soft' eyes.
   - Get yourself grounded and centred. Take three slow, gentle breaths – in for a count of four, out as gently as you can for a count of six.
   - Feel the quality, the texture, the essence of the kind of power you'd like more of.
   - Imagine you are feeling it, sitting in your 'centre', just below your navel, sitting gently halfway between your skin and your spine.
   - Then bring your image, object, or representation into the focus of your intention and take a very small step towards it.
   - Pause for another three breaths, then give a nod of gratitude.

4. Then, gently move away to make yourself a cup of tea, then jot some notes about your understanding of and relationship with powerlessness and power.
5. Repeat this process every day for six consecutive days.

Entry 44: Traditional power and transformative people power

By Dave Andrews

The politics of love involves developing a strong yet gentle power with people. This kind of power is not power that is exercised over people but, rather, power that people exercise over themselves. The power that is strong yet gentle with people is essentially a power that comes from within a person or a group of people.

Looking inwards at how we use power among ourselves

However, nearly every time I talk with people about developing a project in their community, the conversation quickly shifts from discussing internal sources to external sources of power. If they want to organize a welfare programme, they need to discuss funds. If they want to organize a protest movement, they want to talk 'numbers'.

These reactions reveal that people, both on the right and on the left of the political spectrum, believe that external resources matter more than internal sources of power. They believe that politics is essentially all about fundraising and 'number crunching'.

Yet most efforts to bring about change in society don't come unstuck because the groups involved lack the funds or the numbers. Most come unstuck because of power struggles that cause the groups to self-destruct. Hence, the most important single political issue in bringing about change is for groups to internalize an approach to power that enables them to manage their affairs in a way that gives everyone a fair go.

A transformational approach to political power

We need to discard the traditional approach and adopt a transformational approach to political power.

The traditional approach to power can be defined as the desire to control other people and impose change on them. The transformational approach to power, practised in the politics of love, is best described as taking control of our lives, not by taking control of others, but by taking control of ourselves, and welcoming others to do likewise – inviting, not imposing, change.

The traditional approach to political power is popular because it can bring quick and sometimes dramatic results. But it is characterized by short-term gains for some, and long-term losses for many. Every violent revolution, in the end, betrays the people in whose name it fought its bloody war of liberation.

The transformational approach to political power is unpopular because it involves a slow, unspectacular progression. But it is the only way for groups to learn to control themselves, individually and collectively, in ways that are enduring. Through self-managed, other-oriented processes and structures, we can transcend our selfishness, resolve our conflicts with others, and manage our affairs in a manner that seeks justice for everyone.

Community Praxis Co-op: an ongoing experiment in transformational power

Because of our commitment to transformational rather than traditional political power, when a group of us set up the Community Praxis Co-op (n.d.) in December 1998, we committed ourselves to promoting the politics of love, starting with practising it ourselves.

As a community workers' cooperative, we have provided a collaborative infrastructure for members, associates, and colleagues to form self-managed, other-oriented teams of workers. Mutuality and self-control are the hallmarks of our values.

Our signature grassroots training programme, Building Better Communities, has been run in over 100 locations around our state, helping locals build animated communities in their towns in a way that also fosters this transformational approach to power.

REFLECTION

- What do you think of this way of contrasting traditional and transformational power?
- How can you practise a more transformational approach to power?
- What difference could a transformational approach to power make for politics in your community?
- What can you learn from the Community Praxis Co-op's approach for your community?

Experiment 44

Inviting change

This experiment is a basic reflective practice that can also be adapted to any topic at a future time.

1. Consider a moment recently where you felt the impulse to control someone as opposed to controlling yourself.
2. Make some notes about how and why internal sources of 'power' are important in these situations.
3. Think of a relationship that is important to your future efforts at building a better community.
4. Reflect on how *you need to be different* to invite this other person into the kind of ongoing relationship that can bring transformative change to both of you, and ultimately to your wider community.

Entry 45: Subverting dominating institutions

By Dave Andrews

We may dream of nurturing a great society of small communities, but the world in which we are trying to make our dreams come true is a world dominated by institutions.

Obviously, governments and their agencies significantly influence the entire society. And one cynical community worker I know says, 'Don't vote. You just encourage the bastards'.

But I can remember the joy my Afghan friends had in participating in elections, casting votes for the first time in Australia, and watching their votes contribute to the downfall of a government whose policy of detention had made their lives as refugees a misery.

Institutions that dominate our lives, imposing their bureaucracies on our communities, may seem resistant and impervious to the politics of love, but they are not. Institutions are porous because they depend on the people from the communities in which they are located. Therefore, all institutions can be influenced by the political decisions of the people.

Working for change, indirectly

We have found it is easier and more effective to work for change indirectly rather than directly, so we don't immediately threaten the hierarchies, structures, ideologies, and entrenched cultures of dominating institutions. For example, we might start by developing relationships with people in an institution who are interested in community. We get them talking about what they value about community and encourage them in ways to manifest their vision of valued community within their institution. Then we encourage those allies to experiment with inclusivity, equality, and mutuality, in small ways, on the margins of their institution.

When that experiment yields observable positive community outcomes, we might advocate a small, non-threatening pilot project to be adopted and supported by their institution. And we trust that the politics of love will act as a catalyst to transform the culture of the institution from within.

Being subversive is usually risky

Here's a practice story of this kind of transformative process. In our community, we have a major refugee agency that refers to itself as a 'community' organization but functions as a 'bureaucratic' organization. One day, a worker we knew from the agency asked my wife, Ange, if she knew anyone who could befriend a lonely young refugee woman she was working with.

Ange said she did. 'Who?' asked the worker. 'You', Ange said. 'But I can't', said the worker, 'the agency prohibits having friendships with people we work with'. So Ange said, 'Well, why don't you refer her to one of the young women you share a house with. And if she happens to also connect with you, when she is meeting with them, and you all coincidentally become friends, so be it'.

The worker decided to do this. And the friendship group was such an indisputable success in improving the refugees' mental and emotional health (which was the agency's mandate) that she was congratulated by her bosses, and her approach was incorporated into the agency's story because it worked. Over time, the community dynamics of inclusivity, equality, and mutuality slowly began to subvert the official, dominant paradigm of the agency.

Like in this story, sometimes our job is to gently crack institutions open, just a little bit. This may allow the possibility of the emergence of small but significant expressions of community, which can grow into more transformative processes of indirect and informal organizational change.

REFLECTION

- Do you believe that working indirectly for change is sneaky?
- In what circumstances would you have a problem with that?
- What can you learn from Ange's story about the practice of the politics of love?

Experiment 45

Creating cracks in resistant institutions

This experiment is an imaginal practice, asking you to return to the same topic every day for at least three days, intending to become more creative every time.

1. What institutions dominate your community? Identify three.
2. Reflect on how those institutions stifle the emergence of community.
3. Choose one that you care about. Identify three creative ways that you, if you wanted to, could *indirectly* subvert their dominance.
4. Imagine this for at least three days, each day playing with possibilities that are more and more creative.

Entry 46: Forming alliances to counter the politics of division

By Dave Andrews

The greatest challenges to the politics of love are so-called 'friends' and 'enemies'. So-called 'friends' are those who are like us and act like us. So-called 'enemies' are those who aren't like us or don't like us.

Our conceptions of 'friends' and 'enemies' pose a threat to diverse, inclusive communities, as they often create cliques, form factions, and exacerbate conflicts. To practise the politics of love, we need to cooperate not only with 'friends', but also to find new ways to collaborate with so-called 'enemies'.

Australian Muslim Advocates for the Rights of All Humanity

Many years ago, I lived in Afghanistan and got to know many Afghans. On return to Australia, we advocated for Afghan refugees. Up until the 9/11 attacks, we saw each other as 'friends' yet after 9/11, a divisive public discourse saw us as 'Christians' and 'Muslims' – redefined against one another as 'enemies'.

As a response to this redefinition, I visited the local mosque. I said to the Imam, 'I'm not a Muslim, I'm a Christian, but we both belong to the same Abrahamic family of faith, and in the face of the upcoming storm of propaganda that threatens to tear us apart, I'd like to show my solidarity with you by praying with you this Friday'. So, that Friday, I went to the local mosque to pray.

I searched for a 'Muslim' counterpart with whom I, as a 'Christian', could work to rebuild the bridges of communication between our communities, which the extremists on both sides were blowing up. I found Nora Amath, who invited me to join the Australian Muslim Advocates for the Rights of All Humanity (AMARAH).

From that point on, I partnered with Nora. We decided to undertake all our Christian-Muslim engagements together. The first interfaith event we organized was a meal during Ramadan, where Christians and Muslims came together to discuss prayer and fasting. Instead of lecturing and correcting each other, we listened and learned from each other.

Nora and I have tried to arrange as many authentic, empathetic, and appreciative interfaith engagements as possible. Some meetings have been awful, such as the one we hosted at an Anglican church on 'How Christians and Muslims Can Live in Peace'. We were met by an angry mob with clenched fists, wrapped in Aussie flags, demanding through gritted teeth for Aussies to 'resist Islam'. All we could do was graciously absorb their animosity.

Other meetings have been wonderful, such as a similar event we hosted at a Pentecostal church; this time, we were greeted with a range of questions, which we were given time to answer. At the end of the session, the pastor walked to the front of the church, knelt at Nora's feet, and asked her to forgive him for his prejudice. All we could do was rejoice in that triumph of grace over bigotry.

As a result of our collaboration, I've written *The Jihad of Jesus: The Sacred Nonviolent Struggle for Justice* (Andrews, 2017), which is an activist handbook and do-it-yourself guide for Christians and Muslims who want to move beyond the 'clash of civilizations'.

There are many lines of separation in our world

While this story reflects some of the most significant lines of separation in the world, I'd suggest we do it all the time, along predictable lines. More subtle forms of division invade our thinking, such as our own age cohort versus young or old people; 'white folk' versus all other 'races'; migrants versus nationalists; deserving, aspirational middle-class 'lifters' versus lazy, welfare or working-class 'leaners'; or Christian versus unchristian.

We live in an age when traditional politics escalates this division, and demonizing the 'other' is seen as a legitimate political strategy. In the voting systems of many liberal democracies, politicians go all out in pursuit of the 51 per cent needed to be elected to power, and care very little about what the other 49 per cent think. Australian commentator Phillip Adams calls it the 'dumbocracy'. And, unfortunately, we are all a part of it.

The challenge is to build an alternative.

REFLECTION

- Who are the groups regarded as 'friends' and 'enemies' in the public political discourse in your community?
- How can our 'friends' impede our practice of the politics of love?
- What would be the biggest challenge for you in relating to people who are not like you and who probably won't like you?
- What can we learn from Dave and Nora about the practice of the politics of love?

Experiment 46

Build a bridge and get over it

When our own inner prejudices quietly subvert our best intentions, often the best thing we can do is build a bridge to the people we are 'othering' and find a way to join them in their own world.

1. Identify three groups of people in your community whom you are wary of, those who are not like you and may not like you.
2. Choose the one that is easiest to build a bridge to.
3. Identify the public places where some of those people hang out, for example, ethnic groups at football games, young mums at playgrounds, Christians at church, property developers at school functions, and so forth.
4. Go to one of those places and participate in those activities in your own quiet way, just being naturally you, until one of these people invites you into a conversation.
5. Continue until you have a conversation that is either deep or broad enough to give you an insight you have never had before about what life is like in their world. What is it like to be them, in a part of your community where they are comfortable, and you are uncomfortable?
6. Remember, you can build a bridge *to the edge* of their community, but only they can invite you *into their community*. Wait for the invitation. It may be a small start, but you can build on it from there.

Recipe
Banana bread

Prep time: 10–20 minutes. **Cooking time:** 50 minutes. Makes one loaf.

Previously, Carolyn worked at a post office sorting facility where, she says, 'The job was boring and I had no support. The help from supervisors and conversations with customers are my favourite things about working at the Espresso Train Cafe'.

INGREDIENTS

- 5 small (or 3 larger) ripe bananas
- 397 g of self-raising flour
- 60 g of plain flour
- 1 ½ teaspoons of cinnamon
- 210 g of soft brown sugar
- ¾ cup (168 ml) of milk
- 3 eggs (lightly whisked)
- 75 g of unsalted butter, melted (plus another 25 g for the top)

METHOD

1. Preheat the oven to 170°C/338°F/gas mark 3.5.
2. Grease a 24 cm × 13 cm loaf tin and line with baking paper.
3. In a food processor, blitz the bananas or mash well in a bowl with a fork.
4. Add the milk, eggs, and melted butter to the bananas and blend or stir to combine.
5. Sift the self-raising flour, plain flour, and cinnamon into a bowl.
6. Stir the sugar into the flour mixture.
7. Add the banana mixture to the flour mixture, then stir gently until just combined.
8. Pour the mixture into the lined loaf tin and smooth the surface.
9. Slice a 1 cm deep groove along the top of the loaf, down the middle, but not to the ends, with a sharp knife. Then, pour 25 g of melted butter into the cut and over the top of the loaf. This helps it to rise and cook evenly.
10. Bake in the oven for 45–50 minutes.

Section 12: Endings ...

Over the final weeks of our journey, Peter Westoby once again guides us into a few key topics: two about community building and disasters, one about how the local connects with the global, one about what the deep ecologist and activist Joanna Macy calls 'active hope', and a final one on celebration.

We figured that disasters can't be left out. Creating 'shockproof' and 'resilient' communities is part of the 21st-century deal. And best be prepared. In the same way, contemporary forms of community building grapple with how the local interacts with the global, and how we manage our emotional and psychological tendency towards despair (unless we are relatively uninformed).

Finally, Peter wants us to finish on a strong note. Start well, finish well. Hence, the invitation to celebrate while also recognizing the importance of celebration in everyday community life. So, our final five reflections are:

1. **Communities that are connected do better in disaster**, and our role as community builders is to enhance preparedness, so we don't just scramble when the time comes.
2. **Energy, food, and water preparation** discusses how being prepared is not just about being connected; it's also about doing some work around energy, food, and water supply chains, finding out about existing plans and making sure our neighbours know about them, or participating in – possibly even initiating – some collaborative planning, knowing that the planning process itself is an investment in preparedness.
3. **Local work and global connections** introduces various ways of thinking about our local community-building work, in a context of global interconnectedness.
4. **Active hope and working with despair** introduces wise elder Joanna Macy's work on active hope, and how doing something – anything – can fortify our resolve when we acknowledge the reality that it is all a really big mess.
5. **Celebration!** notes some ways we can all integrate rhythms of celebration into our community-building 'work', sometimes through everyday joy and fun, and then in some more substantial ways that communities celebrate together through festival, ritual, and collective memory.

There are five final experiments to complete the development of your practical skills and embodied understanding.

- **Experiment 47. Three key steps towards being a disaster-ready neighbourhood** outlines three concrete actions you can take now that will significantly contribute to disaster preparedness in your neighbourhood.
- **Experiment 48. Find the existing plans and bring them to life – or create a new one** involves continuing your research into existing plans for the wider area, which includes your neighbourhood, in the event of a disaster, with a focus on food, water, and energy security. Your challenge is to find the plans and bring them to life or create new ones.
- **Experiment 49. Exploring local and global connections around a concern** invites you to choose one of your community-oriented concerns and explore the local and global elements of that concern.
- **Experiment 50. Practising active hope** guides you through a process of acknowledging your despair, talking to someone, and taking one small positive action to bring a little bit of positive change.
- **Experiment 51. Celebrating something – anything!** from this year or from this journaling experience invites you to honour your journey through this journaling and learning process by connecting with others to organize a collective celebration of some kind in the coming weeks.

This brings us to the end of the journaling experience. We hope you have learned new ways of understanding and engaging with your broader community. And we hope you have come to appreciate the emergent nature of community itself, as well as the practice wisdom that enables people all over the world, just like you, to create the conditions in which it can flourish.

Entry 47: Communities that are connected do better in disaster

By Peter Westoby

These next two weeks focus on community and disaster.

We live in an era where there is a growing awareness that disasters are becoming, or have already become, the 'new normal'. It's no longer a case of if, but when.

As a group of authors living in Australia, we are acutely aware that each summer brings the threat of fiercer storms, floods, cyclones, and fires, such as the fires in 2019–20 that ravaged the country, destroying millions of hectares of forest, killing people, animals, birdlife, and leaving the land scorched.

Tsunamis and pandemics are other disasters. Heatwaves now leave a severe strain on more vulnerable members of our community, including non-human members.

So, what can a community-building approach offer in response to these ever-increasing threats?

Street-level relationships

Some of us at the Community Praxis Co-op have been working in recent years around community recovery and disaster-related work. One of the key lessons learned is that, when disasters strike, the relationships that are most important to people are often very local. What makes a real difference to disaster recovery and resilience is being well-connected to people in nearby streets. It's about knowing neighbours.

Neighbours are the first responders, and often the ones that hang in there for the long haul in ways that professional services rarely can (they tend to come and go). In everyday practice, this street-level connection means knowing who has a generator, so people can still charge their phones and remain connected when the power goes down, or who has chainsaws, so fallen trees can be removed if roads get blocked.

Of course, it's sometimes about who's got food or other essential supplies. And, as we all experienced globally during the COVID pandemic, sometimes it's simply about having people nearby with whom we could chat (at the end of the driveway or from the front porch) or someone willing to collect groceries when we can't.

In many ways, disaster preparedness offers a valuable opportunity to connect with people at the street level. Some of our work has involved supporting communities in activating 'community connectors' at the neighbourhood level before disasters strike, thereby nurturing the social capital we have previously written about.

As the title of this week's entry suggests, it's best to have these street-level connections in place before disasters arrive, rather than be scrambling around during or after a disaster.

In our work, these street-level community connectors find creative ways to host gatherings in their streets (a barbeque or street cup of tea) so that a 'tree of connections' can be made, ensuring people are connected to one another. These are invaluable during times of disaster. For my partner and I, this means that, when power goes down in a storm, we can text our neighbours to see if it's just us or everyone and respond accordingly.

Eudlo Connecting

In one of the villages where we've been working, some local people formed a local group called Eudlo Connecting. It's comprised of highly motivated, active citizens who want to be catalysts for forming connections that enable better disaster preparedness and recovery. Eudlo Connecting is part of a pre-existing network of local people who host monthly community dinners and musical events at a local hall.

They have incorporated other activities, such as a cooking group and regular events that bring people together, including a men's support group. Following our disaster-preparedness work in the community, this group has incorporated a disaster-related lens into these events, which fosters awareness of community-level preparedness and regular input into the local newspaper.

Already, people who have lived on the same street for literally decades have been connected, exchanged contacts, and demonstrated a willingness to support one another when floods or fires occur, or when the power is cut off for days.

Starting in your own neighbourhood

Of course, as has been explored in this book in previous months, taking action would not necessarily work if it's a solo idea ('I'd like to get this community more prepared for disaster'). It's about starting conversations with people in the street or neighbourhood and seeing if the concern is shared, or, with some new information, whether it could become a shared concern.

It's also about building relationships with existing groups to discover what else is happening in the community. It includes conducting research on the role of local government or other authorities in the disaster space. Then, using some of the approaches explored previously, a small group could come together and start thinking about creative pathways forwards.

REFLECTION

- What are your feelings about this week's topic? Ambivalent? Urgent? Something to put off?
- Practical questions to ask yourself about your own neighbourhood:
    - How well are people already connected in your street?
    - Is there a well-known disaster or evacuation centre?
    - Do people have emergency plans in place?
        - Where might they take their animals?
        - Do they have an emergency kit (for example, a bag pre-packed with water and other emergency items)?
    - Have people considered the implications of communications, assuming power and/or the internet might go down?
    - Do people have access to the radio so they can stay up to date?
    - Do people know multiple ways out of the neighbourhood (evacuation routes)?

Experiment 47

Three key steps towards being a disaster-ready neighbourhood

This invitation to experiment walks you through four steps forwards that will go a long way towards disaster preparedness in your neighbourhood.

1. First, do some research about what's already happening in your community.
   - What's the role of local authorities or disaster/emergency services?
   - What assets already exist in the community around this kind of preparedness (e.g. evacuation spaces/directories)?
2. Second, conduct an audit of who you know in your street, and who you could reach out to at a time of disaster (as it's coming, happening, and afterwards).
3. Third, consider seeing yourself as a community connector, or notice who is already playing that role, and see if a gathering could be convened to discuss this topic and create a 'contact tree'.
4. Bring people together and map the street, ensuring everyone has at least one other phone number for a neighbour and agrees to check in on one neighbour if something happens (or is threatening to happen).

Entry 48: Energy, food, and water preparation

By Peter Westoby

Early in 2024, I had the good fortune of being invited to speak at the World Social Forum in Kathmandu, Nepal. While there, I accompanied some of the community workers from a delightful non-governmental organization called Sahakarmi Samaj (n.d.), meaning co-worker, which itself signals their approach to community development. The 'co' signifies working with the community, for the community.

A cooperative approach to food security

During one field visit, I sat with 20 leaders of a 2,500-member community cooperative that had been established to ensure food security during difficult times, as well as increase livelihood income for poor farmers. By cooperating, these farmers worked collectively to solve many shared problems.

One initiative involves surplus food being saved in large, fully sealed pottery containers, to only be broken in times of disaster and food insecurity. The grain is protected from all animals, insects, and humidity when stored in these fully sealed pottery containers.

This is an example of a community planning ahead for disaster. It's not about waiting or relying on the government. It's not assuming that supermarkets will always have produce available – after all, didn't COVID teach us that's not the case? The community organized for its own future needs through a cooperative structure, which ensured some level of food security.

Planning ahead is important for the community-building process: it enables

It's very easy to make assumptions about what will work during a disaster. For example, when power goes down – as it often does here in Australia – unless you have a lithium battery charged up, or a generator, you cannot even recharge your phone. And even a charged-up phone assumes the phone towers are still functioning.

The point is that disasters teach us the importance of doing some anticipatory community work, of planning ahead. Do people in your locality know of a central place where they can go? Is there a source of water somewhere, or should water be pre-stocked? How about the most marginalized people, do they know? Who will take the initiative to keep them informed?

There's a saying, 'plans are useless, but planning is indispensable'. I'm not 100 per cent sure who said it – although some suggest it was US President Dwight D. Eisenhower – but the point is clear. In the midst of life, and in particular in the chaos of disasters, plans will rarely go according to how you might imagine. However, the planning process itself will have achieved a great deal. New relationships will have been forged, and new ideas circulated. The planning process triggers households to consider their own situation more carefully. Coordinating mechanisms are more likely to have been established.

For example, in our Hinterland and Glass House Mountains towns region, one organization now coordinates the food drop-offs to firefighters, ensuring it's not a messy free-for-all, where food and drinking water are oversupplied to some firefighters, and undersupplied to others. Such coordination means one local organization might provide food one day, another the next, and so on, ensuring a sustainable food supply, if a fire is burning for days or even weeks.

ENTRY 48: ENERGY, FOOD, AND WATER PREPARATION

REFLECTION

- What did you feel and think about the story of the Nepali cooperative?
- What stories do you know of about such pre-planning in your community?
- What do you think and feel about the saying 'plans are useless, but planning is indispensable'?

Experiment 48

Find the existing plans and bring them to life – or create a new one

This week, we ask you to continue your research around any planning your community has already done around one of the areas of food, water, energy, and so forth in the event of disaster.

1. Pick one of these issues.
2. Find out what's already in place. What plans do exist? Who are the key people? Reach out to them and find out if the plans are still viable and relevant, or if they have become outdated and forgotten plans on a shelf.
3. If you find that a plan is dead, consider how you can help bring it back to life.
4. Or, in areas where nothing has been done, use the ideas of this journal to consider activating something with others in your community around that issue.

Entry 49: Local work and global connections

By Peter Westoby

As we approach the end of this book, we, as a group of authors, hope that you are feeling inspired and more equipped to contribute to community building in your street, neighbourhood, or workplace. As we draw to a close, we consider the importance of thinking and acting through a local–global perspective.

There have been different versions of this idea over the decades. At first, people used to say something like, 'think globally, act locally'. We assumed it was best to have a global understanding of the issues and then get involved locally.

Then it quietly morphed into 'think locally, act globally'. This was a response to a growing recognition that most issues could only be solved systemically at a global level. There was a sense that local action was a mere drop in the ocean. And that might be true.

Then we recognized that both these sayings or mantras were falling into the trap, or fallacy, of thinking in binary or dualistic ways. After all, why does it need to be either/or? Hence, some ideas emerged that brought both together, sometimes with odd words like 'think and work glocally'.

More recently, and more usefully, the work of localization has caught on. Localization recognizes that resilient communities need to build both local systems of culture, community, energy, food security, monetary systems, energy grids, and so forth, and delink as much as possible from globalizing forces, which tend to extract from the local.

Working locally while forging global connections

The perspective we have opted for in this book is simply 'work locally' while forging global connections. Our image of change is like a bunch of grapes rather than a large watermelon. Each grape symbolizes local work: communities forging some sense of self-reliance (not necessarily self-sufficiency, as we live in an interconnected world).

The bunch of grapes symbolizes that communities are connected through strands or webs of relationships. It's not about a blueprint of change, where everyone is doing the same thing. Instead, each community is working on solutions and experiments shaped by their context, relationships, and place.

Yet, the relationships between communities ensure people learn from one another and avoid making the same mistakes. It's not so much that solutions are shared, but stories are shared, which then inform other local solutions.

In contrast, the large watermelon image is about the growth of a big organization or a big one-size-fits-all kind of solution. It's the 'bigger-is-better' approach to problem-solving, an idea that, unfortunately, pervades our cultural thinking but rarely works.

Building community is essentially a local endeavour but can be situated in a global context of interdependence.

ENTRY 49: LOCAL WORK AND GLOBAL CONNECTIONS

REFLECTION

- Which of the phrases or ideas used to describe this local–global connection, if any, resonate with you?
    - How and why do they resonate?
- What are some of the benefits and weaknesses of both the grapes and watermelon models of change?
- Consider some stories you have heard from other communities that inspire you and that your community could (or has) learned from.

Experiment 49

Exploring local and global connections around a concern

As an experiment in practice this week, think of a concern you have, or are working on, and explore the local and global elements of that concern.

1. Choose the concern you will focus on this week. Start jotting notes about the various dimensions of this issue, based on what you have learned through this journaling experience over the last 12 months.
2. It will be best to make a start, then to mull it over in the following days, adding to your exploration as you think of new ways of seeing, new perspectives, new connections, or implications as your thinking grows over the week ahead.
3. Avoid binary thinking (either/or) and consider how you can act locally (even if you already are) while simultaneously making connections that support your efforts.

Entry 50: Active hope and working with despair

By Peter Westoby

Sometime in 2024, I wrote a few sentences that have sounded true in my soul for a while. They sit on my computer, prompting me to reflect daily. They go something like this:

> I increasingly sense that I work with effort, diligence, and responsibility, but lack enthusiasm or a sense of mission, because I no longer believe in the effect of what I do.

It's a truth I have been meditating on for a while. When sharing this sentence with a friend, he replied that I am now working in the space that he and I both call 'soul'. When we talk about the soul, we relate it to the *quality* of what we do, because it matters, rather than focusing on effectiveness, success, and impact. A kind of faithfulness to the work. But I sometimes wonder if my lack of enthusiasm is a sign of despair.

Choosing life

Joanna Macy, one of our wise elders in the field of social change, has spent decades of her life reflecting on the importance of doing what she calls 'despair work'. For her, this entails acknowledging the genuine sense of grief and fear that can overwhelm us all when we are committed to social and ecological justice.

Can we avoid fear and grief? She suggests not. To do so will just be a form of psychic numbing. And in that numbing, our sense of despair will paralyse us. In a sense, she invites us all to embrace our despair.

In acknowledging grief and fear and in embracing our despair, we can then move towards choosing life. It's a choice to focus on being faithful to the cause of life, when so many local and global forces ensure the opposite. Macy calls this work 'active hope', an intentional, action-oriented work. Not wishful thinking. Not waiting for anyone else to rescue us, including some magical technology.

Active hope is readiness to engage

Echoing the great literacy expert Paulo Freire, hope is a meaningless word or idea if it's simply dreaming. Hope only makes sense as an 'active' verb, as being involved, as working alongside and with others to make change happen, however small and experimental (Freire, 1994).

In fact, our collective experience suggests that despair can be brought on by inaction. A lack of action tends to lead to a state of being settled and stagnant. Stagnation of action starves the spirit and soul of life energy. It's like the old wisdom, 'if you are depressed or stuck, the best thing you can do is go for a walk'. There's something potent about walking, about getting active.

It's much the same in community work. The best antidote to despair is not mindless action, but getting involved in some small but necessary way. Soulfully. It's to counter the inner critic that suggests 'nothing is worth doing', or 'nothing will make a difference'.

One of our old mentors and colleagues, Anthony Kelly, wanted to title his seminal work *With Hope and Necessity*, signifying this spirit of the necessity of taking action. Unfortunately, the publisher wouldn't allow the title to be used, as it was not easily marketable or easy to put in categories of search engines, so the book was published in 2018 as *Participatory Development Practice: Using Traditional and Contemporary Frameworks*.

> "With active hope, we realize that there are adventures in store,
> strengths to discover, and comrades to link arms with.
> Active hope is a readiness to engage…"

(Macy and Johnstone, 2012: 35)

REFLECTION

- What is your relationship to despair?
- In the same way, what is your relationship to the idea of hope?
- What do you find nourishing or nurturing when you feel a deep grief or despair about the state of the world?
- What do you think of Joanna Macy's idea of 'active hope'?

Would you consider doing Joanna's online course (https://activehope.training/)?

Experiment 50

Practising active hope

This experiment guides you through a process of acknowledging your despair, speaking with someone, and taking one small positive action to bring about a little bit of positive change.

Of course, as the whole ethos of this journal has suggested, it's best to continue to do this with others, in a powerful group. But we start with you as an individual.

1. Consider something happening in your community or the world that you feel despair about. Acknowledge the despair. Feel it. Don't numb yourself. Even speak out aloud and say something like, 'I feel deep despair about…'.
2. Then, think of someone you could share this feeling with. Aim to have a conversation with them about this issue and your sense of despair.

And then, of course – you knew this was coming – despite the feelings, think about something you could do. One thing. As a sign of active hope! For example, it could be picking up some plastic rubbish if you're feeling despair about environmental degradation.

Entry 51: Celebration!

By Peter Westoby

Celebrating good community work is often forgotten. By the time 'the work' is done, people tend to be exhausted. Perhaps the project has sapped the energy or relationships are a bit frayed at the edges. After all, being active and cooperating with others isn't always easy.

Yet, in our collective experience, celebration is an important part of the cycle of building community. We facilitate the initiation and maintenance of activities and new relationships. There's then a time to celebrate. And not just at the end, but along the way as well.

Re-enlivening the joy and creating rhythm

Celebration is about recapturing and re-enlivening the *joie de vivre* – the joy of living. It is best integrated into 'the work'. It's wise to create a rhythm of work and celebration. Not just the big things, but the little things as well. Community work shouldn't be just hard work. It can, in and of itself, enable this celebratory joy every day.

For example, quite often, as I anticipate heading out for an evening community meeting or a late-afternoon committee meeting, I feel lazy and don't want to go. Yet, I have learned that if I push through, I usually experience this *joie de vivre* during and after the gathering or meeting, particularly if they're healthy groups.

I come away celebrating that I am still involved despite the lack of impetus beforehand. Sometimes, I pause and take a moment to celebrate this experience, to feel into it. After all, we often allow ourselves to feel sadness or despair. Why not the joy and fun!?

An example of a community 'work' celebration I have been part of recently included a public event featuring visual storytelling and shared food, in support of the disaster recovery work mentioned in entries 47 and 48. Rather than just letting the project finish in a whimper, people from across five villages who had been involved decided they would love to get together, hear each other's stories through words and pictures, and celebrate with food and drinks. It was a magical evening, generating energy, fostering new relationships, and sparking excitement about what had been achieved over the previous 12 months.

Communities that celebrate together create community, rich memories, and collective rituals

In addition to highlighting the role of celebration in our community work, it is a powerful indicator of a healthy community in its own right.

Only recently, I was working with a group in which people shared that one of their signs of a healthy community was the space to 'have fun'. It's often the forgotten ingredient to community life and work, and yet, if you take time to think about it, fun is often, along with trust, the glue. Celebration is one way to embody fun.

I lived in the inner-city neighbourhood of West End, Brisbane, for over 20 years. So much good work still goes on in that neighbourhood. It's alive with bonding, bridging, and linking social capital. It's very inclusive. It's generally working for justice. But it also knows how to celebrate.

Highlights include the West End Boundary Street Festival, which features food stalls, music, and plenty of laughter on the main street. Then there's the annual Kurilpa Derby, which includes a procession of people in costume, a race on wheels down the main street, and endless other entertainment. Finally, there's the annual Paniyiri Festival in Musgrave Park (which is itself a sacred site for traditional owners), a festival with Greek migrant origins but which celebrates the full range of the multicultural community.

The numerous beautiful celebrations within this small community are what help give life to and sustain community work efforts. And the rhythm of these bigger festivals, where the wider community comes together in more substantial ways to celebrate together, creates a deep and rich collective culture of ritual and social memory, which West End has become renowned for.

ENTRY 51: CELEBRATION!

REFLECTION

- As we approach the end of this year of reflection (or however you have used this journal), perhaps it's time to pause, look back, and consider what you should celebrate.
- How good (or not so good) are you at pausing, reflecting, and taking time to celebrate achievements generally? Or are you, like most, simply moving on to the next thing?
- What kinds of celebrations take place in your neighbourhood? If the answer is none, there's plenty of potential.

Experiment 51

Celebrating something – anything!

Our final experiment asks you to think of something you have been a part of this year that you, alongside some others, might like to celebrate. Any excuse is a good excuse. It's the process that is important.

If you have been a part of a group supporting one another to engage with using this journal over the 12 months, then the 'thing' might well be celebrating this effort and achievement with those people.

1. Pick the 'thing' and choose some people you'd like to celebrate it with.
2. Invite those people to come to your place or convene at a park or another location where you can have a good time together.
3. Celebrate that 'thing'. Invite people to share stories of what they have enjoyed, and what they have got from it.
4. Take a photo or two.
5. Plan to have some homemade cookies (see the recipe at the end of this section) or a homemade cake as part of the celebration, and also some choice drinks.

Recipe
Co-op classic choc chip cookies

Prep time: 20 minutes. **Cooking time:** 24 minutes. Makes 15 small biscuits (or seven large).

We sell oodles of these delicious biscuits at our Nundah Co-operative cafes and often have a selection of variations on the classic. The new favourite is caramel chocolate chips, but a combination of white chocolate and macadamia nuts is just as popular. You can freeze or refrigerate the dough balls and cook in small batches for freshly baked biscuits when the urge arises.

Our member workers with cognitive disabilities are usually tasked with making these tasty morsels. Ali is one such worker, who reliably attends his baking shift every Monday. He works alongside one of our hospitality supervisors or sometimes a social work student. Ali is proud of his contributions to the cafe. While he has tried other jobs, Ali always seems to find his way back to Nundah Co-operative. He takes his work seriously and enjoys spending time at the cafe with colleagues and friends when he's not working.

INGREDIENTS

- 170 g of unsalted butter, softened
- 1 cup (250 g) of brown sugar
- ½ cup (100 g) of caster sugar
- 3 cups (500 g) of plain flour
- 1 teaspoon of bicarbonate of soda
- 1 teaspoon of salt
- 2 eggs
- 2 teaspoons of vanilla extract
- 1 ½ cups (250 g) of chips (milk, white, or caramel chocolate, or nuts, or a combination of these)

METHOD

1. Preheat the oven to 180°C/350°F/gas mark 4. Line a flat tray with baking paper.
2. In a bowl, sift both flours and the bicarbonate of soda. Stir in the salt and set aside.
3. In another bowl, lightly whisk the eggs and vanilla. Set aside.
4. Using a kitchen mixer, beat the butter and sugars for 2 minutes.
5. Add half the dry ingredients to the butter mixture. Mix on low until combined.
6. Add in the egg mixture and combine on a low speed.
7. Add the remaining dry ingredients and combine. Do not overmix.
8. Fold in the chocolate chips or nuts.
9. Divide into 60 g balls or use a damp ice-cream scoop, spacing them 5 cm apart. Do not flatten (during cooking, the dough will spread).
10. Refrigerate the dough balls for at least 1 hour (longer if possible).

11. Bake in the oven for 24 minutes.

You can tell when they are ready as they will start to brown around the edges. Cook for a longer time for a crunchier biscuit or for a shorter time for a soft, chewy one. You may want to check them at 18 minutes because every oven is different. If they're browning around the edges, they should be done. If they are cooking unevenly, spin the tray for the final few minutes to ensure even cooking.

Conclusion

The conclusion uses the genre of dialogue, an approach that is consistent with the ethic and ethos of community building proposed in this book.

We sat in a circle in November 2024, after a day of individual writing, and listened to one another answer five questions. We recorded the conversation. Sometimes, people added to what was previously said. Other times, someone had a completely different thought.

We had set up the circle with the two principles of 'listen with attention' and 'speak with intention'.

Subsequently, Peter, as editor, transcribed what was said and added a light editorial touch. The five questions were:

1. As you have evolved as a practitioner, what's become more important to you in your community-building practice?
2. If a young person asked you what is the one wisdom you'd like them to remember, what would it be?
3. What's the biggest challenge for community builders?
4. What brings you energy or hope in the work of community building?
5. What have you learned from the process of writing this journal?

1. As you have evolved as a practitioner, what's become more important to you in your community-building practice?

Howard: It's about being present with people. Earlier on in community work, you tend to think about the 'doing': what you do in or with the community. But now I think much more about *being with* people, being present, and at times this means doing nothing.

Richard: My thoughts are similar to Howard's. There's an old community-building wisdom by Les Halliwell [a teacher of community development at the University of Queensland], bounced around in Australia, 'Go to the people, listen to the people, trust the people', and in my work it's getting clearer, particularly as I get into positions of management, that you need to remain connected to the people, close to the people, or it's easy to go off track and do something not helpful for them. And by people, I mean the most disadvantaged, the most downtrodden, the most excluded, whose voices need to be magnified. This continues to prod me and teach me.

Kristy: What I've learned lately is to slow down, as I often go too fast and forget to stop and listen. Slowing down allows me to be present and really identify the nut of the problem or issue.

Rachael: I agree with Kristy, it's the slowness, how slow this work really is. And, building off you, Richard, the next sentence of that Les Halliwell prose is 'love the people'. And sometimes that's not easy, but I think it's the crux of it – how to show up with love for the people.

Dave: I think the most important thing is taking the time, being present, being patient, and being supportive.

Peter: Les Halliwell is one of our key teachers; Anthony Kelly is another, and one of his sayings is that 'We have two ears and one mouth, and we should listen at least twice as much as we speak'. And I think that, as I evolve, listening is becoming increasingly important. And listening deeply without leaping to quick assumptions. My wisdom is, 'Meet people, let go of assumptions, and hear their story'. The key then is to simply listen, which of course isn't simple.

Gerard: Honouring my own introversion. Accepting its limits. Acknowledging its strengths. Designing collaborative group processes that are structured, so everyone has an opportunity to participate.

2. If a young person asked you what is the one wisdom you'd like them to remember, what would it be?

Kirsty: Honestly, for me, it's quite simple. Turn up.

Howard: Be present. Similar to turning up. You can't do this from your keyboard, or from the office, and certainly not from your living room watching TV. You have got to be out and about in the community.

Richard: And I'd add that you can't do it alone. It's not about *my* project. It's *our* project. This is a lesson you have to learn over and over again for the rest of your life because we're all addicted to our egos, but we can all break out of that ego-orientation when in a relationship.

Peter: I agree with all of this, but I would add 'Go find a mentor who will walk with you, someone who has skin in the game themselves'. You can indeed learn from experienced hands.

Rachael: I'd invite them to remember to sustain themselves in the work. It's slow work, and if you're not taking care of yourself, you'll definitely burn out. Linked to this is prioritizing who you are and how you turn up. Not just what you are doing, but who you are being. This is so crucial. We can put a lot of energy into our work, but a lot needs to be done within ourselves to bring presence, love, and to take care of ourselves in the process.

Dave: My key wisdom would be 'Do the next thing you can do, no matter how big or small, to make things better in your community'.

Gerard: Your intention is held in the smallest moments. The way you hold a door open for someone and silently invite them to enter with you sets the tone for all that follows. Building community sometimes feels like it takes a long time, but it begins in these everyday, incidental moments.

3. What's the biggest challenge for community builders?

Howard: I think it's 'othering'. Don't be afraid of differences. Particularly when people are different to you. Differences can get you in touch with your own fear, concern, and anxiety, but you need to go there and embrace and understand one another. In a world of much division and polarization, we need spaces where we can engage with people who are different to us.

Rachael: Like Howard, I think polarization and how it creates division is the biggest challenge right now. I think it's a struggle for us all to engage in dialogue and listen to those who hold strongly opposing views. In this political climate, it's even more challenging and important. It's essential that we do not contribute to the polarization and divisions growing in the world.

Kristy: Conversely, it's a challenge to accept others for what they bring, working with their talents and trying to put the pieces of the puzzle together of gifts.

Richard: The biggest challenges are some of the systems we're working in. The large, powerful social systems that encourage individualism and competitiveness. That's a big challenge – working in that world. The beauty of community building is that we're working within a framework much broader than that narrow view of things. So, we don't have to work within the existing systems, but we can work outside, or create new systems, or on the edge of it, in all sorts of creative ways.

Peter: With a sense of all the issues needing addressing, it's tempting to think more action is needed. But what's needed is slow, careful work – how you're going to do a marathon piece of work and make change, not sprinting. That sense of overwhelm leads to a feeling of 'I have to do more', which can result in manic action. And that's the problem. More and more people are manic.

Dave: To overcome my own inertia.

Gerard: Leading from behind the process. Understanding when our leadership is to let others lead. Honouring their clumsy efforts. I had a colleague once who never finished a sentence. At first, I thought them inarticulate. Then I realized they were always making space for the people they were relating with, to step in and take the conversation where they wanted it to go.

4. What brings you energy or hope in the work of community building?

Richard: It's really listening and being with people, and actually getting out of yourself and out of your fixed point of view and opening yourself up with curiosity and opening yourself up to new ideas through relationships, which create whole new horizons. This always brings me hope.

Howard: Two things really give me hope. The first is children, and how they can view the world in simple, non-complex ways and how they can be present. I wonder if that's what Jesus meant when he said, 'you have to become like a child'. The second thing is whenever I am part of a group – for example, last week I was at a gathering at my local community centre, and what a great group they are – and I feel part of a movement with friends doing wonderful things in this community.

Peter: I often sit at home and feel despair. However, there's no antidote to despair like sitting with a group of people and feeling the enthusiasm that comes from engaging in lively conversations. That's what keeps me going, attending a group or workshop. The enthusiasm gives me a spark.

Rachael: The problems are getting bigger; the crisis is growing. But people do keep showing up individually and together. People with huge challenges in their lives – even those who have experienced trauma – keep turning up, working together, caring for each other, and the planet. People haven't given up. Being part of this collective effort gives me great hope.

Dave: My hope is inspired by my faith, a belief in a better world and the better things I see in the community.

Kristy: I am energized when I see what I do making a difference.

Gerard: It's those moments when there is a simple, honest congruence and resonance with someone I am working alongside. A mutual meeting of eyes. A *we* that we both own and value. In this moment.

5. What have you learned from the process of writing this journal?

Rachael: Writing has deepened my practice. And practice deepens my writing. I really love the opportunity to stop, pause, reflect, read, and think, and without this project, I might not have done that. It's helped me see my own practice (how I do things).

Richard: Similarly, it's so important in that writing helps you to stop and really reflect and consider what's important, and that's really helpful. I imagine it could be like this for people journaling – distilling what's important about the entries and how to act.

Dave: Saying the same as Rachael and Richard, writing helps me clarify what I think and reflect on how I feel about community building.

Howard: I'm still distilling what it has meant for me. I am a keen learner, and the writing process has helped me think more deeply about my community-building approach. I've come to realize that writing is actually a form of learning, not just getting thoughts out of my head. It's an experience I am warming to. I have not done as much writing as I could have, but I am learning.

Kristy: I am learning, not as a professional community worker, but in living it every day. I've contributed the recipes but, in reading the sections, I feel the affirmation that I am living it. I am surrounded by it. My wife, a social worker, discusses it. But it's been nice to have this writing on the side, beyond work and family.

CONCLUSION

Gerard: It's all really simple, in the end. Subtle, but simple. All these practices that I learned from colleagues and friends who had tried and tested them before me. They are subtle, but they work. They honour our intention. They hold their own kind of internal rigour, regardless of how clumsily we do it.

Peter: And perhaps this is a useful final comment. This book is just like a community-building process. In community building, you start with individual stories – their dreams or concerns – and then you come together into a small group, and you have to find the shared collective voice. This book is much the same. There are seven voices (seven contributors) and we have had to work out how to find the collective narrative thread. It's challenging to hold each voice, uniquely, but then something shared – a shared voice. I hope the reader can hear both – the voice of each writer with their own values, perspective, and style, but also a collective voice with a broader, overall set of values, perspectives, and style.

References

Introduction

Cameron, J. (1992) *The artist's way: a course in discovering and recovering your creative self*, Jeremy P. Tarcher/Putnam, New York.

Jenkinson, S. (2018) *Come of age: the case for elderhood in a time of trouble*, North Atlantic Books, Berkeley, CA.

Section 1

Bonhoeffer, D. (1954) *Life together: the classic exploration of Christian community* (translated by J.W. Doberstein), Harper and Row, New York.

Minimalist Baker (n.d.) 'Banana bread granola'. https://minimalistbaker.com/banana-bread-granola/

Proteus Initiative (n.d.) 'About us'. https://www.proteusinitiative.org/about-us

Section 2

Andrews, D. (1996) *Building a better world*, Albatross Books, Sutherland, NSW.

Block, P. (2008) *Community: the structure of belonging*, Berrett-Koehler Publishers, San Francisco.

Community Praxis Co-operative (n.d.) 'Community Praxis Co-operative'. https://www.communitypraxis.org

Couchsurfing (n.d.) 'Couchsurfing'. https://www.couchsurfing.com

CREATE Foundation (n.d.) 'CREATE foundation'. https://create.org.au

hooks, b. (2003) *Teaching community: a pedagogy of hope*, Routledge, New York.

Peck, M.S. (1987) *The different drum: community making and peace*, Simon and Schuster, New York.

Putnam, R.D. (2000) *Bowling alone: the collapse and revival of American community*, Simon and Schuster, New York.

Westoby, P. and Dowling, G. (2013) *Dialogical community development: with depth, solidarity and hospitality*, Tafina Press, Brisbane.

Section 3

Andrews, D. (1996) *Building a better world*, Albatross, Sutherland.

Buber, M. (1937) *I and thou*, Bloomsbury, London.

Gyatso, T. (14th Dalai Lama) and Cutler, H.C. (1998) *The art of happiness*, Easton Press, Norwalk, CT.

Kelly, A. and Westoby, P. (2018) *Participatory development practice: using traditional and contemporary frameworks*, Practical Action Publishing, Rugby.

Westoby, P. and Dowling, G. (2009) *Dialogical community development: with depth, solidarity and hospitality*, Tafina Press, West End.

Section 4

Food Connect Shed (2025) 'About us'. https://www.foodconnectshed.com.au/about-us

Schumacher, E.F. (1973) *Small is beautiful: economics as if people mattered*, Blond and Briggs, London.

Kelly, A. and Westoby, P. (2018) *Participatory development practice: using traditional and contemporary frameworks*, Practical Action Publishing, Rugby.

Add in online bible ref

Section 5

Lederach, J.P. (2003) *The little book of conflict transformation*, Good Books, Intercourse, PA.

Nhất Hạnh, T. (1999) *The heart of the Buddha's teaching: transforming suffering into peace, joy and liberation: the four noble truths, the noble eightfold path, and other basic Buddhist teachings*, Broadway Books, New York.

Peck, M.S. (1987) *The different drum: community making and peace*, Simon and Schuster, New York.

Tuckman, B.W. (1965) 'Developmental sequence in small groups', *Psychological Bulletin*, 63(6): 384–9.

Tuckman, B. W., and Jensen, M. A. C. (1977) 'Stages of small-group development revisited', Group & Organization Studies, 2(4): 419–427. https://doi.org/10.1177/105960117700200404

Section 6

Leunig, M. (2006) 'In the company of strangers', *Sydney morning herald*, 17 August.

Mackay, H. (2018) *Australia reimagined*, Pan Macmillan, Sydney.

Putnam, R.D. (2000) *Bowling alone: the collapse and revival of American community*, Simon and Schuster, New York.

REFERENCES

Section 7

Kaur, V. (2020) *See no stranger: a memoir and manifesto of revolutionary love*, One World, New York.

Louv, R. (2012) *The nature principle: reconnecting with life in a virtual age*, Algonquin Books, Chapel Hill, NC.

Shiva, V. (2005) *Earth democracy: justice, sustainability and peace*, South End Press, Cambridge, MA.

Ward, M. (2011) *The comfort of water: a river pilgrimage*, Transit Lounge, Melbourne.

Section 8

B Lab (n.d.) 'Certified B corporations'. https://www.bcorporation.net

Glassman, B. (2006) *Instructions to the cook: a Zen master's lessons in living a life that matters*, Free Press, New York.

Nenquimo, N. (2024) *We will not be saved: a memoir of hope and resistance in the Amazon rainforest*, Wildfire, London.

Schumacher, E.F. (1973) *Small is beautiful: a study of economics as if people mattered*, Blond and Briggs, London.

Self-Employed Women's Association (SEWA) (n.d.) 'About SEWA'. https://www.sewa.org

SevGen (2025) 'Home'. https://www.sevgen.com.au

Solnit, R. (2016) *Hope in the dark: untold histories, wild possibilities*, Haymarket Books, Chicago, IL.

The Schumacher Institute for Sustainable Systems (n.d.) 'The Schumacher Institute'. https://www.schumacherinstitute.org.uk

Section 9

Andrews, D. (2021) *To right every wrong*, Wipf and Stock, Eugene.

Benarrawa Community Development Association (n.d.) 'Benarrawa'. https://www.benarrawa.org.au

Russell, C. (2020) *Rekindling democracy: a professional's guide to working in citizen space*, Citizen Network Research, Sheffield.

Street Up (n.d.) 'Street Up'. https://www.streetup.com.au

World Health Organization (2025) 'From loneliness to social connection: Charting a path to healthier societies', WHO Commission on Social Connection. https://www.who.int/groups/commission-on-social-connection/report

Section 10

ABC (2016) 'Baby Asha: protesters vow to put bodies on the line to prevent baby's offshore removal', *ABC News*, 21 February. https://www.abc.net.au/news/2016-02-21/protesters-vow-to-block-cars-if-baby-asha-isdeported/7187278

Clark, D. (1975) *Basic communities*, SPCK, London.

GROW (2025) 'Mental wellbeing programs'. https://www.grow.org.au

Hatch, P., Ireland, J. and Booker, C. (2015) 'Royal Children's Hospital doctors refuse to return children to detention', *The Age*, 10 October. https://www.theage.com.au/national/victoria/royal-childrens-hospital-doctors-refuse-to-return-children-to-detention-20151010-gk63xm.html

Reconciliation Australia (n.d.) 'Reconciliation Australia'. https://www.reconciliation.org.au

Uluru Statement (n.d.) 'The Uluru statement from the heart'. https://www.ulurustatement.org

Section 11

Adams, P. (2016, January 23). 'That's dumbocracy', *The Weekend Magazine, The Australian*. News Corp Australia.

Andrews, D. (2015) *The jihad of Jesus: the sacred nonviolent struggle for justice*, Wipf and Stock, Eugene, OR.

Andrews, D. (2017) *Building a better world: developing communities of hope in troubled times*, Morning Star Publishing, Melbourne.

Community Praxis Co-operative (n.d.) 'About us'. https://www.communitypraxis.org/about-us.html

Love Makes A Way (n.d.) 'Love makes a way for asylum seekers'. https://www.facebook.com/LoveMakesAWayForAsylumSeekers

Section 12

Freire, P. (1994) *Pedagogy of hope: reliving pedagogy of the oppressed*, Continuum, New York.

Macy, J. and Johnstone, C. (2012) *Active hope: how to face the mess we're in without going crazy*, Finch Publishing, Warriewood, NSW.

Sahakarmi Samaj (n.d.) 'Sahakarmi Samaj'. https://www.sahakarmi.org

www.ingramcontent.com/pod-product-compliance
Lightning Source LLC
Chambersburg PA
CBHW061206070526
44583CB00025B/3128